EMOTIONAL CIVILITY

The New Standard For Global Success

By

Dr. Sharon Anderson

Live To Produce Publishing Group Mesa, AZ 85212

FOREWORD

Dr. Sharon Anderson is the foremost leading voice in the world today on the subject of Emotional Civility. She is a prolific writer on this subject with a keen insight to the practicality and functionality of emotional civility. This book awakens new pathways of thinking. I like to call this Functionality that opens doors to new information to enhance your life. I wonder how many people's lives would be different if they had opportunity to understand the concept of emotional civility before they committed the actions that put them in a compromising position.

Dr. Anderson's is truly number one in this civility narrative of Emotional Civility. The entire planet needs to read this book, because the information within these pages will empower any individual or organization to operate at the top level for peak performance in every area of life. Productivity will increase as people begin to understand the concept and the philosophy of emotional civility. I will make the bold prediction now.

This book will be a Global bestseller.

Thank you, Dr. Sharon Anderson, for leading the world into a new paradigm of civility called emotional civility: the "Mother" of this global initiative to empower the world.

Sir Clyde Rivers World Civility Leader

INTRODUCTION

In a time where civility seems to have vanished, the purpose of this book is to remind us of the powerful concept to not allow our emotions to control our speech or our conduct. My book, "Emotional Civility: The New Standard for Global Success" is designed to place at the forefront of our daily interactions the value of civil interaction that ultimately will bring peace and safety to our homes, communities, and nations. In 2020 in the United States, we were on the brink of war with Iran; witnessed two impeachment hearings, endured a global pandemic, observed numerous instances of police brutality ending in the death of black and brown people of color and witnessed the most uncivil standard of communication in decades in the hallowed halls of Congress; culminating in an attempted insurrection and coup. I am calling for us to hit the reset button. We are in a constitutional crisis because of a lack of civility in our discourse.

It is my hope that after reading this book we will be reminded that we can disagree without being disagreeable; that we can seek the common good; that we can do the hard work of staying present with those whom we have deep rooted and fierce disagreements so that disagreement does not turn into disaster. It is my hope that parents with young children are reminded of the true standards of civility that this great nation was built upon, and call out and correct and mentor their youth to firm but fair speech. The goal in writing this book is for the reader is to develop emotional (and spiritual) stamina so when an offense occurs, we don't react out of emotion but out of wisdom. The goal is to encourage the reader to examine where they are on what I call the "civility spectrum" and assess their responses and interaction on that spectrum, and to turn down the heat when it seems like the only response is harsh and hurtful. It is my prayer that this book has such an impact on the reader, that civility and a civil response becomes the norm and not the exception in their life and in our world.

ACKNOWLEDGEMENT

I would like to dedicate this book to my heroes: my parents – James and Jacquelyn Styles; for they have been and were true examples of the exercise of emotional civility in my life. It may be hard to believe in this era, but I was blessed to grow up in a home where civil discourse was REQUIRED! You talked it out with respect! Yelling, screaming, and name calling were not tolerated. In fact, I only remember witnessing one argument among my parents, who were married for 48 years before my Father passed in 2006. I was taught to take the high road, not to sweat the small stuff, to avoid conflicts at all costs, and to not reduce myself to discourse that was unprofitable. My Father would remind me to "always be a lady" and my mother was the model of that behavior. As you can imagine, once I hit my 20s, I was not 100 percent successful in this effort – and have had a journey professionally and personally where I did the exact opposite – and justified an emotional and uncivil response with me "being real," "telling it like it is," and "giving someone a piece of my mind." I now know, and I am very aware, that in many instances had I responded differently to certain things and in various situations the outcomes may have been different. There were consequences. I thank Almighty God for Grace, and my Lord and Savior Jesus Christ. Without Him I am nothing. Thank you mommy and daddy, and my big brother Curtis. It is because of you, that I am! It is because of the importance of your teaching that I write this book. It is because of you that I focus on Emotional Civility as a commitment and an area of study and thought leadership in hopes that this book will serve as a reminder of the importance of graceful interaction and civil speech and the discourse that you required of me, and that you exemplified.

I also would like to acknowledge my Pastor, Bishop Glen Staples, presiding Bishop of the Temple of Praise, who also, through an example of civility, spiritual humility, wisdom and strength, taught me so much about adjusting to different environments as a professional. I am thankful that he fathered, loved and mentored me through some of the most challenging moments of my life. Thank you, Prophetess Deborah Webb, my spiritual mentor who encourages and prays for me daily – and has no problem with correcting me when I get off track. To Tena Loving, my rock, confidant, and best friend for over 50 years, I could not do life without you. Thank you, Tena, for always being there in EVERY up and down I have experienced. Finally, to Ambassador Clyde Rivers and Dr. Lady Nakia Wright. Thank you for recognizing the giftings in me and God's divine timing to push me to write this book NOW. All of my work experiences, and life lessons, from being born in New York City to growing up in Suburban New Jersey, to studying international relations at Tufts University and law at Georgetown University Law Center, to working for the Mayor of the District Columbia, to serving as an Associate and Executive Pastor at the largest church in Washington, DC collided to birth this manuscript. Your discernment and constant push catapulted me to my now! A special thanks to my publisher, Dr. Vernet Joseph for the tweaks, and adjustments – and patience.

Lastly, I dedicate this book to my children and grandchildren, Collin James, Kyle Dee, Jameka Danielle, Gia Iman and Caiden Jose, Daniel Bradley, and Jalyil Abraham (and God children – Jordan Loving, Pastor Ikisha Cross, and Tia Diggs). You are leaders, trailblazers, and nation changers. I write this because I want a better world for you! I write about Emotional Civility to encourage you and all leaders to become better examples of true leaders! If no one else, I write this book for my beloved children to help you understand your emotions, keep them in check, and to teach you how to be and remain civil in action, word, and deed. You make me proud!

TABLE OF CONTENTS

CHAPTER ONE

THE BIRTH OF EMOTIONAL CIVLITY

"You get more bees with honey"
"Peace is not the absence of conflict, it is the ability to deal with
conflict by peaceful means." – Ronald Reagan

I struggled to complete a cross examination of a psychologist in a juvenile homicide case. My tactic: sharp toned, aggressive, sarcastic, even a little harsh. I mean, wasn't that what a good cross examination should be? However, the strategy was not working. I could not even get the psychologist to give me undisputed and simple information, let alone get her to admit or buy into facts that were helpful to my case and client. What was I doing wrong? The judge sitting on the bench was constantly rolling his eyes at me with every harsh, sharp tongued, but adeptly worded question. Whew, it was time for a lunch recess, time to re-group, time to re-assess my strategy.

Well, the break came, the jury and witness were released from the courtroom, and I was left alone with the Honorable Judge Robert Scott (may he rest in peace). Judge Scott was not known to be the most civil of judges in the halls of District of Columbia Superior Court. Indeed, quite to the contrary, he was very critical of attorneys, and often publicly rebuked and embarrassed them if they were not competent in his eyes. He was infamous for calling you out in front of a jury if you were not performing to the highest standards as a trial lawyer. On the other hand, he respected qualified and competent attorneys, and gave you a fair trial if you "knew what you were doing." Fortunately, I was one of the few attorneys that Judge Scott respected. As I was about to exit the courtroom for lunch, still puzzled by why my cross-examination strategy was not working, he called me to the bench, and growled, "STYLES" (he always called me by my last name) "YOU GET MORE BEES WITH HONEY" and he stormed off the bench and out of the courtroom. What on earth was he talking about? What did he mean? I was already frustrated by my inept cross of the psychologist, and it was such an odd statement; what did bees and honey have to do with a murder case? Then it hit me! My cross-examination! I was questioning a professional, and my tone and demeanor were combative and aggressive and downright uncivil. Change the tone-get the information-win the case. A light bulb went off: you do not have to be "cross" to cross-examine a witness. Know your witness, understand your purpose. I changed my tone; I won the case. Hence, my journey and interest in the study of civility and professional decorum was birthed.

As indicated in my acknowledgements, my parents were the hallmark of civil decorum. However, life in the 80s and 90s took me on such a journey that I had strayed far, far away from the tenets of the Styles household. The bees and honey analogy pushed me to really examine the role of civility in all aspects of our existence. Over a decade before the concept of Emotional Intelligence (EI) was

2

birthed I became a scholar of civility, writing about the concept of civility in the courtroom. In 1995, while teaching at Howard University Law school, I had the pleasure of co-authoring a law review article on civility in the legal profession with Professor Andrew Tastlitz (also now deceased). The article, "Still Officers of the Court: Why the First Amendment is No Bar to Challenging Racism, Sexism and Ethnic Bias in the Legal Profession," published in the Georgetown University Law Review, was my first scholarship on civility in the legal profession. My research and studies revealed evidence of a wide range of discriminatory conduct by lawyers and judges to each other and witnesses. Objectionable conduct ranged from glass ceilings facing female attorneys to ethnic slurs intimidating or infuriating opposing attorneys and witnesses. Therefore, how or if I respond to various situations or conversations has been a professional focus ever since. Trust me, my path has not always been the most pristine or successful in following the rules of civility. However, my upbringing in the face of what I was learning from society often seemed to clash and nudged me to examine and focus on this area of scholarship and thought.

When I answered my call to minister and preach the gospel of Jesus Christ, my degree path took me from an earned juris doctorate from Georgetown University Law Center to an earned doctorate in Pastoral Counseling. Pastoral Counseling is a unique form of psychotherapy that has the option of using spiritual resources as well as psychological understanding for healing and growth. Pastoral Counselors have in-depth religious and/or theological training and thus can address psychological and spiritual issues. A "pastoral approach" implies gentleness, patience, and a lot of listening. As I pursued my profession (which may be seen as bi-vocational) as a lawyer and pastor, I made an effort to teach and model civil responses in the face of adversity, embarrassment, anger, hurt, disappoint, and discouragement. The two professions, however, can often be seen as polar opposites. As a lawyer firmness and aggressiveness are the keys to purported success. However, as a Pastor, I began to study and look at civility from a spiritual perspective and was drawn to write this book; as we say "For Such a Time as This." Hence, the concept Emotional Civility (EC) was born. The concept of Emotional Civility was so revelatory that the National Archives awarded my request to have society recognize and dedicate a day to celebrate Emotional Civility. Consequently, on March 6 of every year we now are reminded that civility matters, and we are encouraged to practice emotional civility – on that day especially – but every day!

I am thankful to have aligned and partnered with the "Father of Civility", Dr. Clyde Rivers. Dr. Rivers and his IChange Nations movement are committed to *bringing back the lost art of honor* by building a Culture of Honor that recognizes individuals throughout the world who have exemplified extraordinary humanitarian efforts to effectively change nations. At IChange Nations, Dr. Rivers honors people and organizations that believe every life is valuable and is created to bring a contribution to the world. ICN is the largest "building cultures of honor" network in the world. Dr. Rivers and his commitment to Civility for All and his global movement of World Civility is gaining tremendous momentum daily. This book is a step in my committed partnership with Dr. Rivers to help fulfill a life-long mission of treating all of humanity with respect and living the Golden Rule.

CHAPTER TWO

EMOTIONAL INTELLIGENCE VS. EMOTIONAL CIVILITY- WHAT IS EMOTIONAL CIVILITY

"So, let us begin anew – remembering on both sides that civility is not a sign of weakness, and sincerity is always subject to proof. Let us never negotiate out of fear. But let us never fear to negotiate." – John F. Kennedy

I was a Senior in College. I had studied in Spain the semester before and earned enough credits to graduate early. I chose to write my thesis for honors and worked at home. Back then, we did not have the internet and computers. We used typewriters, carbon paper, and white out. Every week I sent my work to my thesis Chair. Every week I received great comments on my progress. Then the time came to defend my thesis in person. I drove the normal 6 hours from New Jersey to Medford, Massachusetts. I was excited about it. I was ready. My team (who I selected) included the new African American Professor in the Political Science Department; my favorite English Professor, and the Head of the International Relations Department. I arrived and when I sat down I was told by the head of the Department that we would not be going forward that my work had not been accepted. My Chair, the new African American Professor, would not look me in the eye. My English professor looked away. I was stunned! Devastated! I excused myself and walked to the stairwell and cried my eyes out. There were no cell phones back then so there was no one to call. But my Father's words rang loudly through my mind and my spirit. You are enough! NEVER LET THEM SEE YOU SWEAT! THINK BEFORE YOU SPEAK! So, I gathered myself, and I returned. Instead of "giving them a piece of my mind," I confidently explained that I was appalled that after months of work without critique that they would take this action. In a calm tone I told them that I believed it was racially motivated. I told them that I would not challenge the decision, and would graduate with my class – albeit without honors. I drove back to NJ with my head high! I chose civility in the face of a situation that in many ways deserved a COMPLETE CUSS OUT and an EMOTIONAL RESPONSE! I was disrespected and devalued. However, in that situation, my quiet protest was my success. I went on to work for the CEO of IBM, and then on to Georgetown Law School. Since then, my career and professional path have been phenomenal, and I am proud and thankful to say that my career decisions have had positive impacts throughout the nation. Many of my students are judges, own law firms, head non-profit organizations, and are leaders in their professions. There were many times when exposed to racism, sexism, and misogyny that I wanted to quit and/or act in a manner that would have led to a huge uproar and momentary satisfaction. But my path and growth may have been stunted, which in turn may have affected my impact on those that went ahead of me and came behind me- had I failed to act with emotional civility. Thinking before speaking and acting is critical to success.

Emotional Civility

So, what is Emotional Civility? For scholars, it may be quickly confused with Emotional Intelligence. We have all heard of the term and the study of emotional intelligence or EQ or EI. Emotional Intelligence (EQ) is defined as the ability to identify, assess, and control one's own emotions, the emotions of others, and that of groups. In 1990, Daniel Goleman, in his role as a science reporter at *The New York Times,* chanced upon an article in a small academic journal by two psychologists, John Mayer and Peter Salovey. Mayer and Salovey offered the first formulation of the concept they called "emotional intelligence." The phrase *emotional intelligence,* or its casual shorthand EQ, has spread to the far corners of our planet, and the application of EQ principles has been utilized in the workplace, halls of academia, and in the areas of leadership and employee development. *The Harvard Business Review* has hailed emotional intelligence as "a ground-breaking, paradigm-shattering idea," one of the most influential business ideas of the decade. The concept and study of EI has changed my life and caused me to become more diligent, and be more cognizant in managing my emotions and focusing on my responses. So much so that I began to teach EI as a consultant. I have taught a course for middle level managers in DC Government surrounding EI in the workplace, and now look at ways to promote civility as a standard response in our lives, globally. There is a difference between Emotional Intelligence and Emotional Civility. Emotional Intelligence is vertical and relates to how you process your emotions and the output based on your emotions. Emotional Civility is horizontal and addresses the impact of your response based on emotion. There is a bridge that is built between individuals that ensures emotionally civil responses. That bridge can be built with understanding, tolerance, and the components of civility. That bridge can also be obliterated with the issues that undermine true civility for all (racism, misogyny, privilege, and inequality). It is important that we examine the work we must do as individuals to ensure that the bridges we are attempting to build – do not get torn down- because the bricks we are using are unstable, outdated or misinformed.

Civility is the basis or Platform for EI and EC

Civility is courtesy in behavior and in speech. The great John F. Kennedy said that despite common belief: Civility is not a sign of weakness, and sincerity is always subject to proof. Civility means a great deal more than just being nice to one another. Civility costs nothing, and buys everything. Civility is not a tactic or a sentiment. According to Tomas Spath and Cassandra Dahnke, Founders, Institute for Civility in Government, civility is claiming and caring for one's identity, needs and beliefs without degrading someone else's in the process. President George Washington in his publication, *Rules of Civility and Decent Behavior in Company and Conversation*, offered an instruction that included "every action done in company ought to be with some sign of respect, to those that are present." We must proceed with civility. There is no doubt we live in a world that constantly turns to violence over peace and incivility over civility. However, if there is anything our great leaders of change have shown us, it is that we are stronger together and stronger when we are kind. Incivility drives wedges through our society that truly keep us from achieving our full potential. It prevents us from having an open mind to all ideas, maybe even the one that just may be the very change needed to make our world a better place.

8

Emotional Civility

Emotional Civility (EC) DEFINITION

Taking the general concept of civility a step further, I define Emotional Civility as the space or lane between your head and your heart, the moments between when something hits your gut (your heart, your spirit) and when you decide whether or not to respond, (text, hit the like button, decide not to hit the like, tweet, etc.) improperly. EC is the lane where you decide to not throw a punch or pick up a weapon and shoot.

EC is not just the response, it is the work you do and the choices you make between the stimuli and the response to ensure that the response (verbal, written, or behavioral) is civil. Like EI, the skills of EC are listening, tolerance, and asserting one's views in a manner that does not involve tearing down the views of others – no matter how unpleasant or different they might seem. I will readily admit that those who practice EI in their lives are most likely to also produce civil responses or act with Emotional Civility. However, Emotional Civility requires that people communicate with respect, restraint, and responsibility. Emotional Civility is the recognition of the need to act with civility and the commitment to do so when circumstances may scream otherwise.

In the personal example that I cited above, when after working diligently to earn an honor for graduation by writing a thesis focused on international communication I was rejected because of race, the circumstances screamed that I should have given them a piece of my mind. I had every right to "lose it" but I did not and I left with my own self-respect. I had a right to fight the decision appropriately. What I did not have the right to do was scream, holler, and act unprofessionally. To further illustrate EC – picture a four-lane highway, and then picture an exit ramp. That exit ramp represents

EC. It is the choice you make in various situations to act with civility-not just based on your emotions and how your response will affect you- but also on how it will affect others. This book examines the different circumstances we all find ourselves in that may spark or provoke an emotional reaction. Oftentimes we are so deeply engrained in a moment or circumstance or an emotion that we do not even realize that we are acting in an emotional manner that may end in destruction; a destruction in a relationship, career, etc. When we act or react emotionally there are consequences. Some consequences take years or even decades to outlive. There are some consequences from which you may never recover.

CHAPTER THREE

THE HISTORY OF CIVILITY IN AMERICA AND AROUND THE GLOBE

"Civility is claiming and caring for one's identity, needs and beliefs without degrading someone else's in the process."
– Tomas Spath and Cassandra Dahnke, Founders, Institute for Civility in Government

Before we examine Emotional Civility, I think it is important for us to revisit the history of civility in America and in the law. My background as a law student and law professor at three top tier law schools in the country (Lecturer of Law Appointment at Harvard Law School, Visiting Associate Professor at Georgetown Law School and Associate Professor at Georgetown Law School) compels me to take a brief look at the history of civility in America in the context of the emotional civility paradigm. We must ask ourselves: What is civility? Based on where we are in society, it is clear that there is profound confusion about what it is and why there is a need for such a review. As we look at the events and violence on the stage of the United States of America in 2020-2021 – unfolding as if it was a scene in a movie, in our country that

11

was once hailed as the pinnacle of democracy -- it is clear that a brief civility lesson is warranted.

The word "civility" originated in the late 14th century. Civility comes from the word *civis*, which in Latin means "citizen." Merriam Webster defines civility as civilized conduct (especially: courtesy or politeness) or a polite act or expression It refers to the "status of a citizen," from Old French civilite (14c.), from Latin civilis "relating to a citizen, relating to public life, befitting a citizen; popular, affable, courteous" (see civil). Later especially "good citizenship" (1530s). Adolf G. Gundersen and Suzanne Goodney Lea have developed a civility model grounded in empirical data that "stresses the notion that civility is a sequence, not a single thing or set of things." Civility actually goes beyond good manners and listening attentively. Civility includes sharing our own beliefs and values with others through some type of engagement with the intent of sincere respect towards one another. Civility requires a willingness and open mindedness to having our opinions and biases challenged by others who share a different and perhaps completely unique perspective and points of view. Emotional Civility like Emotional Intelligence takes it a step further. It recognizes that the ability to act with civility is deeply connected with our ability to understand our own emotions. Understanding our own feelings helps us to recognize how we are feeling in real-time and gives us a greater ability to have empathy and understanding for others. Understanding our own personal feelings can help us to evaluate the things that trigger us emotionally and, therefore, become more aware and in tune with how we can, could and will possibly react and feel in certain situations. By being open to taking the time to understand our thoughts and emotions in these situations, this practice can lead to the self-recognition and acceptance of how the same or similar situations may affect others, including those that may share a completely unique perspective. THIS IS EMOTIONAL CIVILITY. Practicing emotional civility requires thoughtful behavior and continuous refinement of our perceptions of what matters to us and to others. It takes work in the face of disappointment, discontentment, pain, grief and misunderstanding. Practicing civility in good times and happy times and feel-good times is not the challenge. The challenge is practicing civility when you feel or are experiencing the exact opposite. THAT IS EMOTIONAL CIVILITY.

CIVILITY AND PEACEFUL PROTESTS

While yelling and shouting may seem effective (and sometimes, they are), don't let anyone tell you that quiet but passionate gatherings don't leave a mark. There are numerous peaceful protests throughout history that made a difference, and we're still talking about many of them today. In fact, I think that the peaceful protests are largely more effective: There's something powerful about a group of people fighting for what they believe without actually fighting. That is Emotional Civility at its finest.

It goes back to the comforting saying that has become particularly famous as of late: Love trumps hate. You can't conquer fear with fear. Negativity with negativity. Anger with anger. Love, passion, understanding, forgiveness — these are traits that drown out all of the bad.

Even as far back as 494 B.C., peaceful protests were used to spark the flame of change in the face of injustice. The Conflict of Orders was a series of largely nonviolent and bloodless protests organized by the plebeians, who were working, lower class Roman citizens.

They were protesting the current social structure put in place by the government, which was dominated by patricians. Patricians were an extremely privileged and high class of Roman citizens, a class only achievable by birth. These protests lasted from 494 B.C. until 287 B.C., when the system was finally replaced with an aristocracy based on the holding of political office, wealth, and property. Each set of protests brought the plebeians more rights, protections and access to public offices. Finally, in the early 3rd century, plebeians received equal status, although they were still at a considerable disadvantage in terms of wealth and prospect within society. This series of protests were some of the oldest we know of in history and a reminder that people have always attempted to inspire change through organized movement using emotional civility.

The United States Civil Rights Movement

This peaceful protest came down to the simple act of refusing to ride the city buses of Montgomery, Alabama for 15 days. Those who participated did it to protest segregated seating. It was considered the first large-scale protest against segregation led in the United States. Just four days prior to the boycott beginning, Rosa Parks had been arrested and fined after refusing to give her seat up to a white man. Ultimately, the Supreme Court ordered the city to integrate the bus system. The protest also brought into the spotlight Reverend Dr. Martin Luther King, Jr., the Civil Rights movement's infamous leader and, in my view, an icon of emotional civility for us to always follow when we measure and examine peaceful protesting. Dr. King emphasized the need for emotional civility and ability to make a strong point without using harsh and negative or hurtful language or conduct. Dr. King was the example of how to communicate anger, hurt, frustration loudly BUT peaceably without violent or hurtful rhetoric. Emotional Civility was demonstrated on August 28, 1963 when more than 200,000 people gathered around the Lincoln Memorial in Washington, D.C. They were there to protest segregation and demand equal rights for all. Dr. King gave his infamous "I Have a Dream" speech and the peaceful protest, in large part, sparked a change in the nation, passionately reminding us that all people are created equal. Given the harsh treatment of African Americans (from slavery to the lynching, dog attacks, use of water hoses and beatings) an uncivil response would certainly be understood. But the leaders of the civil rights movement understood the power of peace – of emotional civility – and the choice to respond with civility – even in the face of incivility. Emotional Civility helped to ensure the passing of the CIVIL RIGHTS Act requiring equal treatment of all Americans. The quality that set Dr. King apart and made him successful was his civility. Emotional Civility was the methodology that revolutionized Dr. King's movement towards equality. In a time of violence and war, Dr. King led the movement of peaceful protests. His silent sit-ins spoke significantly more words than one loud or patronizing statement could have ever made. In a time when things were far from civil, Dr. King discovered the large and crucial cooperation between productivity and civility.

Women's Rights

On March 3, 1913, Lawyer Inez Milholland Boissevain led more than 5,000 people down Pennsylvania Avenue in Washington, D.C.. This peaceful march – exhibiting emotional civility – became one of the most monumental events in granting the right to vote to women, and the National American Woman Suffrage Association raised more than $14,000 to fund it. The right to vote wasn't granted to women until seven years later with the passing of the 19th amendment, but this peaceful parade is still considered pivotal in the final decision and step in the direction toward legislation in support of women's rights. While discrimination against women was a charged issue, the path toward equality was paved with emotional civility and communicated with peaceful protests.

Sports Figures and Civility

At a medal ceremony during the 1968 Summer Olympic Games, two African American track runners stood atop the medal podium, fists raised high and heads bowed. Runners Tommie Smith and John Carlos had just won medals for their athletic performance, but instead of simply basking in the glory of their success, they took the opportunity to bring awareness to the dehumanization of African Americans in the United States – an issue that desperately needed (and still needs) attention. During the Olympic games, racial inequality and injustice were thriving in the U.S., despite the international boasting of being the home of the free and the brave. While the U.S. national anthem played, Tommie Smith and John Carlos stood with black-gloved fists raised high above their bowed heads. They later explained that they bowed their heads as a sign of respect for the country; however, some people back home did not feel the same way. Millions of viewers from the U.S. were outraged, and when the Olympians returned home, they were vilified by their own country. They protested silently with emotional civility. However, it should be noted that emotional civility does not always produce a reciprocal response with emotional civility.

Tommie Smith explained in an HBO documentary that "[They] were just human beings who saw a need to bring attention to the inequality in our country." He went on the explain that he did not like the idea of people looking at what they did as negative. Mr. Smith further explained, that there was nothing but a raised fist in the air and a bowed head, acknowledging the American flag not symbolizing a hatred for it. On the one hand the activity, a shocking, yet peaceful protest, inspired viewers from countries all around world. This peaceful display reminds us that moments of success can provide us with a platform to bring awareness in creative and emotionally civil ways. However, it is important to remember that we cannot control how others will respond to us and how we communicate. Even when we make the right choice to act and communicate peaceably-others may not agree with the stance we take. Quiet protest may still be met with public and aggressive response. What is important to highlight is that these athletic icons chose to use emotional civility in their simple but powerful gesture. Again, with all instances of discrimination the opportunity, and justification, for fighting, yelling, screaming is forever present and available. But these men stood silently with their fists raised and exhibited emotional civility. As a result, we are still talking about the significance of their gesture today.

Most recently, we again witness the power of emotional civility in the social justice arena. Colin Kapernick, an NFL football player, former quarterback of the San Francisco 49ers has certainly been an icon and example of emotional civility. Colin Kapernick, frustrated by unequal treatment for the black race and police brutality, took a knee during the National Anthem to protest the numerous shootings and killings of unarmed black men and women and children in the United States. Like Tommie Smith, he used his status and influence in sports to bring awareness to the issue. The response to his peaceful protest has been mind-blowing. He was blackballed from the NFL, criticized by the former President of the United States

Donald Trump and called an expletive, and condemned for his silent stance against an obvious crisis in our society. Many fellow football players and politicians (mostly white) reflecting on Kaepernick's protests felt the "the country wasn't ready" for the important message the quarterback wanted to send.

It is interesting to think that a public figure in the 20th century in the United States of America could be condemned and harshly treated for calling out social injustice, especially around police reform, PEACEFULLY. His colleague and fellow football player Alex Smith said of Kaepernick in an interview that, "Nobody was ready for it, and he's sitting there trying to tell everybody through a completely peaceful manner about some of the things going on in this country that had been going on for a long time." Certainly the statement provokes the question -- "When will we ever be ready?".

It is curious to think that the United States of America was not ready for the peaceful manner of one expressing themselves against injustice, particularly when there is a historic outline of Americans utilizing peaceful protests to bring attention and awareness to issues of unequal treatment. Peaceful protest/emotional civility is something that we have attempted to engage in for over 100 years. Yet today, in 2021, there has been a grave attack on civility like never before. That is why this book is needed. That is why Emotional Civility Day is necessary. That is why the reminder to return to acting with civility has been launched with fervor and intention. Not everyone will respond with civility to civility. But that is the goal of this book, is to encourage us all to continue to use civility and make an effort to respond with civility – even in the face of the harshest circumstances.

The George Floyd Protests

The George Floyd protests were an ongoing series of protests against police brutality and racism that began in Minneapolis in the United States on May 26, 2020. The civil unrest and protests began as part of international responses to the murder of George Floyd, a 46-year-old African-American man who was killed during an arrest after Derek Chauvin, a former Minneapolis Police officer, knelt on Floyd's neck for 9 minutes and 29 seconds as three other officers looked on and prevented passers-by from intervening. Derek Chauvin and the other three officers involved were later arrested. On April 20, 2021, Chauvin was found guilty of second-degree unintentional murder, third-degree murder, and second-degree manslaughter.

The George Floyd protest movement began hours after his murder as bystander video and word of mouth about it began to spread. Protests first emerged at the East 38th and Chicago Avenue street intersection in Minneapolis, the location of Floyd's arrest and death, and other locations in the Minneapolis–Saint Paul metropolitan area of Minnesota. Protests quickly spread nationwide and to over 2,000 cities and towns in over 60 countries in support of the Black Lives Matter (BLM) movement. Polls in summer 2020 estimated that between 15 million and 26 million people had participated at some point in the demonstrations in the United States, making the protests the largest in U.S. history. While there were a number of instances of looting and some arrests, the protests began as a peaceful cry against the epidemic of police brutality against black and brown men and women in the United States.

The Struggles of Civility Throughout the Globe

Across the globe there are numerous and powerful examples of peaceful protests and hallmarks of emotional civility. In New Zealand the deforestation of the Puerora Forest had finally upset one too many people because companies and the government were decimating the wildlife and polluting the natural landscape due to their logging operations. To protest the deforestation, hundreds of people went into the forest, built tree houses, and refused to leave them. The deforestation couldn't continue with people amongst the trees. The government permanently stopped all logging operations, and the area was ultimately turned into a park. The Puerora tree sitters, as they were later termed, inspired other similar events against deforestation. We can think of a number of different ways those in opposition to the deforestation could have responded, yet they chose emotional civility, and the outcome was successful.

Across the globe there is an outcry and a sense of urgency and need for ensuring civility in every nation- which makes this book and insertion of the emotional civility paradigm into our society so important. In India, it has been said that incivility is on display in Indian politics for three reasons 1) The rampant use of 'unreason' in the democratic polity (i.e.– concepts that promote that cow dung can absorb harmful radioactive elements); 2) The language of the political leaders are frequently derogatory and political leaders are stooping down to the lowest levels to seek votes in the elections. The use of derogatory and filthy remarks for one's political opponent has become a new normal in Indian politics. The language of political discourse in India's polity displays its brazen incivility; and 3) The rise of majoritarianism in India has created an atmosphere of fear in which mob lynching and detention of advocates of human rights has become a new normal. The dominance of money and muscle power in the political arena also refers to the kind of incivility India has been able to actualize. Civility can only prevail in the absence of fear. Peace and security are a precondition for civility. Many say that fear and lack of equity and security is governing politics in India- and is the prime example of incivility.

Fundamental civic rights, including freedoms of association, peaceful assembly, and expression, has deteriorated across Africa in 2020. In its latest annual report, the CIVICUS Monitor an online platform that tracks civic freedoms in 196 countries, downgraded four countries in West Africa. Côte d'Ivoire, Guinea, Niger and Togo have all been downgraded from the "obstructed" to "repressed" categories, meaning that people in these countries face serious restrictions when trying to exercise their fundamental rights. Over the past year the CIVICUS Monitor has documented several drivers of civic space violations in Africa including mass protests that were met with violent repression, and electoral processes, mostly presidential elections. Violations in the context of elections often involve the arrest of opposition members and pro-democracy activists, internet shutdowns, detention of journalists and crackdowns on protesters.

In three of the four West African countries that were downgraded Cote d'Ivoire, Guinea, and Togo – constitutional changes were adopted in recent years, leaving incumbent presidents Alassane Ouattara, Alpha Condé and Fauré Gnassingbé all claiming that new constitutions allowed them to run for further terms. The process of changing constitutions or bypassing term limits led to mass protests that were met with excessive force, the adoption and use of restrictive legislation, and punishment for dissenters criticizing those in power, in particular pro-democracy activists.

Niger has also been downgraded by the CIVICUS Monitor. Even though a peaceful political change of power seemed likely at the time of the drafting of this manuscript, serious questions remain about Niger's democratic prospects as human rights violations continue and civil society is subjected to restrictions. These countries in West Africa have not been alone in efforts to muzzle dissent, exclude opposition and crack down on protests in the context of elections. This bleak picture is further seen in Eastern and Southern Africa.

In Burundi, ahead of the May 2020 elections, state security forces and members of the youth league of the ruling party threatened, intimidated, and killed opposition party members, and stifled the media and civil society organizations.

In **Tanzania**, as the country prepared for its August 2020 vote, the government embarked on a major crackdown to suppress dissent, including by enacting new laws and regulations to stop opposition members from actively campaigning, prevent civil society organizations and independent observers from observing the electoral process, weaken civil society and the media, and limit the use of online platforms by journalists and voters. Despite this difficult picture, the year also proved the resilience of people and civil society in exercising their civic freedoms, leading to fundamental democratic changes.

In Malawi, although the period surrounding the disputed May 2019 election was characterized by violations including internet shutdowns and repression of protests, civil society successfully contested the results, leading to a new election and a change of government in June 2020. Unfortunately, many other African countries are moving away from holding free and fair elections. With several countries gearing up to hold elections in the coming months, civic rights violations are being reported in countries across the continent.

In Uganda, opposition members and their supporters are being violently prevented from holding rallies and journalists are being arrested and violently attacked while covering events held by opposition candidates and civil society; human rights defenders are being threatened by state authorities, including by having their bank accounts frozen and their operational licenses withheld.

In Ethiopia, civil society groups have expressed concern at the crackdown on dissenting political views ahead of the general elections slated for 2021. Similarly, in Zambia, civil society has denounced an escalating trend of judicial harassment, repression, and attacks on human rights defenders ahead of the August 2021 general elections. In Benin, electoral laws have been adopted that make it difficult for opposition candidates to stand in the 2021 presidential election, which might lead to President Patrice Talon running almost unopposed. The situation is so bleak that for the first time in a decade, according to the 2020 Mo Ibrahim Index of African Governance, overall governance in Africa has declined. The Index highlighted that, "in terms of rights, civil society space and participation, the continent had long before embarked on a deteriorating path and the pandemic simply aggravated this existing negative trajectory."

Given that this book is not a history book, I will stop here. The summaries and instances of incivility are overwhelming. All countries, including the United States have experienced and are experiencing a civility crisis in politics and in society. In my view the pandemic created a level playing field. The world was shut down. We finally are more alike than different. As a result, this book is for all nations. Civility – Emotional Civility must be a new standard for global success and must be practiced at all levels – so that we can realize our collective and individualized goals for peace and civility throughout the world.

CHAPTER FOUR

THE CAUSES OF INCIVILITY

"Civility is caused by a person's emotions or lack thereof. If a person is emotionally affected by the negative feedback that they get from other people in a psychologically normal manner then they are defined as civil." – Dr. Alveda King

C ivility is defined by acting in a normal manner when affected by negative feedback. Emotional Civility is the intentional awareness of one's emotion and the work required to ensure a civil response to negative input of feedback. Its civility and emotional civility that looks at a "normal" response, then when addressing such circumstances, the first question we must examine is what is normal? We must also look at how negative the feedback is or the input that one is responding to when deciding if the manner of response is "normal" and then civil. While everyone is different, and everyone's level of tolerance is different, I have found in our "normal" interactions there are many instances that cause us to veer off from emotionally civil responses if we are not grounded in how we are handling our emotions. Any property owner knows that even a small leak in a pipe has the potential to do massive damage over time. Caught early, a leak won't ruin much. Ignored long-term, it could cause the roof to cave in. Headline-grabbing,

25

egregious examples of bad behavior may seem like the equivalent of a burst water main. However, they're usually the end result of less noticeable, small issues that were not resolved or addressed when first noticed. We can never control the input, but we can control how we respond. Failure to control your emotions in the face of negative behavior like rudeness and unfairness, steadily destabilizes your ability to exhibit EC one drip at a time. In this chapter, I outline a few emotionally charged issues that we all face as individuals, and that require a particular focus during our journey of examining emotional civility.

RESPECT

R-E-S-P-E-C-T find out what it means to me/ R-E-S-P-E-C-T taking care of TCB. The infamous song by Aretha Franklin, an anthem of women worldwide. Respect is something earned and yet demanded. Respect and Civility are often used interchangeably. When we think of civility and respect we often return to the "Golden Rule," "Treat others as you would like for them to treat you." The Rule, while easy to remember, is often more difficult to apply in the face of disrespectful circumstances. That intentionality of care and respect for others is the critical "oil" that helps our community, in all of its diversity, to run smoothly. When one person fails to consider the effects that his or her actions can have on others, and does not act intentionally with civility and compassion, the quality of life in an entire community is degraded, perhaps just a little, but those acts of inconsideration and incivility can add up. As we demand respect, EC asks the question – What do you do when respect is not given or honored? Emotional Civility not only requires that you treat others with respect, but it also requires the harder task of acting civilly in the face of incivility. There are thousands of young black men who are incarcerated because of what they deemed a lack of respect. A look, a statement, a step on a toe, etc. The response was disproportionate to the level of disrespect or incivility. Think of the number of young men who could be graduating from high school or college or law school or medical school if they were taught about emotional civility and taught to take that exit off the EC spectrum to a more civil response to disrespect. EC rejects vengeance – because vengeance belongs to the Lord. EC rejects an eye for an eye. EC is what Michelle Obama penned when she said, "When they go low, we go high!" That is emotional civility. EC is what Hillary Clinton did after losing to Donald Trump. They laughed at Hillary Clinton – found taking long hikes in the woods with her husband and dogs after losing a long and hard-fought political battle to Donald Trump. Who could ever forget the time when Donald Trump disrespected her during the debate by circling her on the stage prowling, stalking, and looming like an animal ready to pounce? EC was Hillary Clinton continuing her composure and not responding to the provocation. That is EC. It goes without saying that we should be respectful of everyone we encounter. It is when we are disrespected that it is so difficult to turn the other cheek and respond appropriately. Individual and global success is dependent upon us always being the bigger person. That is the penultimate measure of emotional civility. That is when it matters.

PATIENCE

Impatience is often the cause of incivility and acting with patience is a hallmark of EC. A short fuse is the cause of lack of EC. Impatience can prevent you from standing in someone else's shoes. Our impatience or the quality of not wanting to put up with or wait for something or someone causes us to perpetuate uncivil responses. Our society craves instant gratification. We like things to happen right away. We like results. Waiting is just not something most of us are not good at, and it can be a problem and a cause of incivility, since most things in life happen to take time. We live in a microwave generation. We want everything instantly and when we don't get it when we want it – we react. Once again looking through the lens of EC, EC requires us to act with civility when someone lashes out at us with impatience. Do you respond with incivility when someone lashes out at you with impatience? Again, is an eye for an eye, tooth for a tooth appropriate? When looking through the EC lens the answer is a resounding NO. We live in a world when a store representative or cashier lashes out at us or someone behind us complains about us in a line in the grocery store. The instances of road rage that have ended in death – ended tragically not just because of the stimuli but the response to the stimuli. What about as parents when our children cry out "Are we there yet? "as we travel to a long-awaited destination. Do we scream at the little ones for acting with predictable impatience, or do we look for ways on the EC spectrum to defuse our irritation at the stimuli and choose the more civil response? EC is the ability to walk away. EC is counting to 10 before we respond. EC is the choice to accept wrong. If Derek Chauvin had acted with EC relating to George Floyd he would not have remained on his neck for over nine minutes. If Derek Chauvin had acted with EC he never would have arrested George Floyd and George Floyd would be alive. EC is the response of a peacemaker.

LOVE /KINDNESS/TOLERANCE/CHOICE OF WORDS

Acting with EC causes us to look behind the harsh output from another in order to best manage our emotions and responses. I was watching an episode of the infamous television show "This is Us." In this particular episode the character Toby was camped out in the hospital parking lot tailgate style awaiting the birth of his adoptive daughter. Emotions were high in that he and his wife Kate were not sure if the birth mother, upon seeing her newborn baby, would change her mind about the adoption. While Toby is seated in the parking lot, an older man pulls up demanding that Toby get out of "his" parking space. The old man is rude and intolerant. Toby tries to explain how inconvenient it would be for him to move – and certainly describes how the parking lot is full of open spaces – yet the older gentlemen is unyielding. Toby could have flipped him off, yelled, and cursed him out, but instead Toby asks the older man why this particular parking space, in a field of open parking spaces, is so important. He then learns that the older man's wife, Rose, is in the hospital on a ventilator due to Covid and may not live. Parking space 1570, the space Toby was occupying, was the space that the old man parked in every day to wait outside the hospital in hopes that Rose would not die and be taken off the ventilator. The number 1570 it turns out was Rose's favorite number. Toby and the older man shared their fears and joys. They ended up supporting one another while waiting for news of a positive or negative outcome. This episode displayed a prime example of EC and modeled civil behavior. Toby took the time to understand the frustration, rudeness, and intolerance of the older gentlemen. How many of us would have held onto that parking space like a piece of real estate? How many of us would have argued over a parking space never really taking time to understand why the other "claimer" felt the way that they did? EC requires us to look at our responses from the perspective of another. When we do so the results are kinder, gentler, and safer responses to situations, and a more tolerant society.

Please understand I am not advocating acceptance of abuse. I believe in the concept of legal self-defense (defending yourself when you are in imminent danger of bodily harm) if the amount of force used is consistent with that harm. I also believe in standing up for what you believe in. I am a strong black woman who is known for advocating passionately for what I believe is right. However, using profane, abusive, vulgar, or harassing language; berating or criticizing people in public; or belittling people who are different or think differently is not acceptable. We observe in our news everyday instances, of verbal abuse by political leaders, and for years witnessed in the workplace individuals who have experienced the backlash of angry e-mails or text messages, which is a clear form of incivility. Lack of tolerance for difference of opinion has caused the spread of incivility throughout the world.

Other instances of incivility include: talking negatively about others; interrupting conversations; passing along rumors or gossip; embarrassing people publicly; yelling, fist pounding, phone slamming, throwing objects; chipping away at someone's self-esteem through constant slights; undermining another person's work; constantly making minor, irritating putdowns; and addressing people in an unprofessional manner are all examples of unacceptable behavior and examples of incivility that are common experiences in our society. The list goes on and on. We cannot and should not tolerate incivility of any kind. We must speak out against any aspects of abuse of any kind. However, emotional civility requires us to examine how we will act if exposed to this negative behavior. The purpose of this book is to remind us that we cannot control how others communicate and emotional civility is about how we individually control our own emotions and respond the right way; or respond with values undergirding civility even if we are approached in a hostile or abusive manner.

EXPECTATION BREEDS RESENTMENT

Despite what your common sense may tell you, research shows that people are surprisingly inept at predicting how we will feel in various situations. Our expectations can get the better of us when we expect more than what is realistic in a given situation. A wife knows her husband has been under a lot of stress lately, so she decided to surprise him by making one of his favorite dinners. But for all her labor, all the wife gets back from her husband is a mumbled, "Thanks for making dinner" and little else. The wife is disappointed and hurt. She expected overwhelming gratitude and a change in her husband's demeanor. Not only is she disappointed, she is now resentful. She starts slamming the drawers as she cleans up the kitchen. Now she is mumbling and huffing and puffing. Many wives and husbands can relate to this scenario. Look up the word "expectation" in a dictionary and you'll find two definitions. The first is about expectations that signify your belief about what someone should do. You expect your kids to clean their rooms once a week or not hit each other. You expect your partner to be reliable, pay the electric bill when he or she says they will, or be honest or faithful. Our expectations can create significant stress when they don't match up to reality. Also consider how social media can greatly contribute to this: we compare our own worst moments (those not deemed to be shareable online) to others' best moments, which very often are filtered to seem perfect. We may not even realize this mismatched comparison.

In a professional environment we also see the pitfalls of expectations. When working on a project how often do we expect co-workers or partners to think like us, or process solutions like us. If someone does not agree, do we make an attempt to understand their view or view them as an adversary? Do we take it a step further and develop a campaign against the individual who simply thinks differently-because we EXPECT everyone to agree with our way of thinking or our solutions? Do we go even further and totally disengage with that individual simply because they just disagree-and we expect everyone to understand our point of view? In real life, such expectations are like ground rules that create the foundation for a relationship and are usually never openly talked about.

The other definition of expectation is the belief that something will happen in the future the way you want it to happen. You plan to go on vacation and have a good time, or you work hard on your job and you'll get a promotion. This is about the future, usually all inside your head and heart. The expected good-time vacation may be a bust because a hurricane comes along and sabotages your plans. You don't get the promotion because the company goes under, or your boss, unbeknownst to you, always planned on promoting someone else instead.

These are the expectations that can trigger an uncivil reaction and is where we often get in trouble. We have an image of what we hope will happen but unlike the cleaning of the rooms, the paying of the electric bill, it goes unspoken. The problem is that the outcome is dependent on a future that we can't control and a person we can't control. We often respond due to the expectation instead of our reality.

But it doesn't stop there. It's easy for such failed expectations to accumulate over time, leading to resentments that can undermine even the strongest relationships and cause the biggest outbursts. Expectations aren't bad in and of themselves; we all have them. They are a natural part of life. The problem arises when we place *too much weight* on the expectations of others, to the point that we start living for their approval or cannot process change well. We get lost somewhere between the way others see us and who we really are – and then our responses become less about who we are and more about what we expect from others. This causes us to crash and burn on the EC spectrum. Instead of managing our emotions, they are completely controlled by what someone else does or does not do. This can lead to depression and low self-esteem and uncivil behavior not only to others, but to ourselves. Yes, we can be uncivil to ourselves. Instead of acting out we act in and create havoc in our head and in our hearts, which can lead to self-destruction.

This is why an examination of emotional civility is so critical. If we begin to examine how we are processing matters internally, externally we are sure to see an improvement in our civil responses in society. Emotional Civility starts with us.

CHAPTER FIVE

THE TOOLS AND COMPONENTS OF EC/ FOUNDATION OF EMOTIONAL CIVILITY

"Civility does not here mean the mere outward gentleness of speech cultivated for the occasion, but an inborn gentleness and desire to do the opponent good." – Mohandas K. Gandhi

In society we do not have "rules" mandating civility, for as a society and community we understand that respect and compassion for others must come from inside of us, from our essential selves. And when they come from "who we are," they become a part of our culture. Unfortunately, today we see that civility has, in many contexts, not been widely put into practice. We see it on social media where people voice negative opinions of others, on the highways where some drive as if they're the only ones on the road, in line at the grocery store where the mother hits or curses at her misbehaving child, on the street where people use coarse language when others can hear, in the park where people carelessly drop their trash, in the college classroom where a student has opted to plagiarize from the work of others, and the sad list goes on and on. If you were to stop those people and ask if they'd want to be the recipients of such treatment, most would probably say "no." It is hoped, when you are tempted to say or do something that could have a negative impact on another person, that you remember the Golden Rule and just ask yourself, "How would I feel if someone did this to me?"

Statistics show that there is a perceived lack of civil discourse throughout our nation. Weber Shandwick, in partnership with Powell Tate and KRC Research, began exploring civil discourse in our public squares back in 2010. Even then, the perceived lack of civility in the United States had far-reaching implications and negative consequences for the nation. Over these many years, and even in the most recent study, KRC researchers have found that Americans continue to report that incivility is harming America's future, our standing in the world and our democracy. From politics to random internet comments, there seems to be more and more rude, demeaning, insulting, and aggressive language and behavior in our society – nationally and internationally. It was only a few short years ago when Pastor Rick Warren attempted to welcome us to the new era of global "civility," and the emergence of a civic "common good" happening at the global level. Pastor Rick Warren was invited to deliver the invocation at President Obama's Inaugural. But critics claimed that to the average American, "civility" was one of those mantra-type buzz words that invokes nice feelings of camaraderie, implying polite disagreements, but destined to become a way to shut off the more polarizing aspects of culture and theology. In other words, critics of civility feel that any attempt at teaching or promoting civility means that you can't express yourself and speak your mind. They cry First Amendment foul. In fact, one of the greatest enemies to civility and civil discourse are the notions of "that is just the way I am" or "that is just how I talk or express myself." This "right" to express one's self, while rooted in the First Amendment, is not without societal consequences.

Indeed, Freedom of Speech is often used to justify the most inappropriate and uncivil discourse, which is, in my mind, offensive to the principles and foundations upon which the First Amendment was built. Just because you CAN say something doesn't always mean that you SHOULD say something. This brings us to our emotional civility spectrum. Where do you fall in filtering your conversations? Do you have a filter? Do you care how people feel after you have had a conversation? Do you feel you have a right to say...WHATEVER and WHENEVER? If you have a right to say WHATEVER, do you have a right to say it HOWEVER? Does your tone and manner of communication matter? Have you had any experiences that caused you to pause or regret your manner of communication?

I certainly have. For those of us who strive to treat people with respect, emotionally uncivil communication happens when you are tired, stressed, upset, embarrassed. The reason why I termed the concept "Emotional Civility" is because it examines our responses that are triggered by emotions. It is easy to respond appropriately when things are going well. It is often when we are not at our best that we respond in ways that we most often regret because we do not, or in some instances refuse to, practice restraint. Not only do we have to monitor what we say and how we say it to promote civility but when we say it is also important to examine. A response is not always called for. (Unfortunately, I fail at this almost daily) Waiting to give comments when cooler heads prevail is always an appropriate option and evaluation when examining civility.

Emotional Civility

According to the most recent studies on Civility in America: A Nationwide Survey, civility in America continues to erode and rude behavior is becoming our "new normal." Incivility has become the default in too many of our interactions and it is affecting the very fabric of society. "Incivility is turning into a national epidemic.

When seven out of ten citizens report that incivility has reached crisis proportions in this country, it is clear that we need new solutions and greater leadership accountability. We may have reached the tipping point" (Civility in America: A Nationwide Survey). Americans don't just perceive incivility; they personally and frequently experience it in their everyday lives. Perception and reality are not that far apart. On average, Americans encounter incivility 17 times during the course of one week, or more than two times per day. Just over four in 10 individuals expect to experience incivility during the next 24 hours. With 24/7 exposure to acts of incivility, it is not surprising that incivility has reached crisis levels. Of great concern is that the majority of Americans believe we have a civility crisis and that uncivil behavior is leading to an increase in violence. However, nothing is being done; the fan of uncivil discourse is being flamed. This book is a reminder of our individual responsibility and some suggestions on how we can work on ourselves to reduce it. Public dialogue often lacks civility and efforts toward policy consensus rarely enjoy broad democratic engagement. Today's hardened lines of political division threaten to aggravate and perpetuate social problems. The need for more effective and successful democratic engagement is clearly seen in the paralysis and acrimony in our state and national governments and violence worldwide.

Given that the studies showing an ever-increasing world where incivility is acceptable and the norm – the tools and components of emotional civility are increasing important. We all too often put on a mask of civility but remain snarky on the inside – having a dialogue in our head about why we dispute or reject what we are hearing another person say. We form judgments, and make decisions based solely on past interactions that lie the groundwork for us yet again to crash a burn on the emotional civility spectrum. That is why the key tool and component of EC is LISTENING.

There are various types of listening which are important to mention as we evaluate the tools of emotional civility.

Active listening is a technique of careful listening and observation of non-verbal cues, with feedback in the form of accurate paraphrasing, that is used in counseling, training, and solving disputes or conflicts. It requires the listener to pay attention, understand, respond and remember what is being said in the context of intonation, timing, and non-verbal cues (body language). This differs from other listening techniques like reflective listening and empathic listening.

❖ Active listeners react to what they're hearing — with nonverbal cues, paraphrasing or repetition, and questions.

❖ Active listening requires full attention and an effort to clarify and understand.

❖ Active listeners analyze what they're hearing and summarize or paraphrase it to ensure they understand. Active listening is key to emotional civility.

Emotional Civility

Passive listeners merely listen. The passive listener doesn't have a part in the communication. Their role is to simply listen. This is ideal for situations where a speaker addresses a group of people or when the listener is enjoying music on the radio, a podcast, or theater production. Unfortunately, in communication that is highly charged, many people practice passive listening versus active listening. As a result, they are reacting based upon misinformation or partial information. Oftentimes an explosion occurs. Listening passively when active listening is required frequently if not always results in emotional incivility.

Active Listening helps us from rushing to judgment about a person and their comments. Active Listening helps restrain the immediate response which is often harsh and inaccurate- particularly when we are discussing charged or emotional issues. Active Listening paves the way for clear discernment and not clouded judgement. Active Listening is the most critical component and tool of emotional civility. If we fail to actively listen – and learn how to actively listen, we will always ultimately fail to offer a civil response.

CHAPTER SIX

INDIVIDUAL COMMITMENTS TO CIVILITY – A MIND IS A TERRIBLE THING TO WASTE

"Civility costs nothing and buys you everything." – Lady Mary Worley Montague

Incivility is the polar opposite of civility, or in other words a lack or completely without civility. Verbal or physical attacks on others, cyberbullying, rudeness, religious intolerance, and vandalism, are just some of the acts that are generally considered acts of incivility. Incivility is a negative part of society that has impacted many people in the United States, but as the world is becoming increasingly more transparent in social interactions, it has become increasingly more apparent that incivility has become an issue on the global stage. Social media and the web have given people the ability around the globe to freely exchange ideas, but it has not come without its consequences. Survey results have discovered that incivility affects an employee's behavior. For example, Porath and Pearson's (2013) survey highlighted that 25% of employees who have experienced incivility contributed fewer ideas and engaged less. A poll of 800 managers in 17 industries was investigated and the phenomenon of incivility indicated that 48% of employees reduced their effort on their everyday tasks, 47% reduced the duration spent on work intentionally and 38% reduction on work quality. Incivility in the workplace cost the workforce billions of dollars each year. Porath, Christine & Pearson, Christine. (2013). The Price of Incivility. Harvard business review. 91. 114-21, 146. The monetary costs of incivility have been estimated to be as high as $14,000 per employee Incivility in the political arena continues to plague America.

Politicians in the U.S. have frequently cited that they encounter a lack of civility in their workplace, and have disregarded it as an unfortunate aspect of politics, but polls indicate that "going negative" can help candidates win elections. During the 2016 presidential campaign, candidate Donald Trump regularly called his rivals "stupid, incompetent and losers." There are so many examples incivility in the workplace and politics that the costs are easily to measure.

Not only is incivility perceived as a problem in America- this perception is indeed a reality in our country. "Your perception is your reality" is a mantra used, that I particularly loathe but have come to appreciate. Every year, perceptions pertaining to America's civility decline is tracked, and the results have consistently found that three-quarters (74%) of Americans believe civility is worse compared to a few years ago. Eight in 10 surveyed point to the risks that incivility has on society as dangerously high; a majority identifies serious ramifications from incivility, including cyberbullying, harassment, violence and hate crimes, intimidation and threats, intolerance, and people feeling less safe in public places.

Moreover, personal encounters with incivility remain high, as 80% of people report having experienced uncivil behavior at one time or another. The frequency of uncivil encounters per week rose sharply in 2018 and remains at that level in 2020, with average Americans reporting experiencing a wide number of weekly encounters as uncivil. Notably, the location of uncivil interactions has shifted over the years. Uncivil online interactions have increased from an average of 4.4 weekly interactions in 2013 to a high of 5.5 in 2019, while uncivil in-person interactions have declined from 5.9 in 2013 to 4.7 this year. It has never been more important to understand the sources and impact of America's eroding state of public discourse as Americans continue to view it as an alarming problem. From consumers in the marketplace and students in schools, to employees in the workplace and voters at the polls, few are immune to our country's civility crisis. That is why emotional civility is so important.

We need to begin to think of civility as continual and non-negotiable. It is not something that we turn off and on when we are ready. Civility is not something we use to beat someone down or rule over another. Because civility was deemed negotiable by our previous administration, our societal norms have been shaped and formed by that conduct. Civility is the one law that has not been applied and has not been given the opportunity to resolve the issues at hand. Commitment to do what is right must prevail in our society. Civil policies must be created and we cannot simply offer lip service to those situations that require civility. We cannot use an old environment for new policies. Difference in opinion will occur, but we must remember that diversity is not adversity. We must care about justice – because justice flows from an emotionally civil society. Justice brings oppression to injustice. We must cry out for civility over uniformity. We must not hide behind the First Amendment as a mask for incivility—the cost is too great!

CHAPTER SEVEN

THE IMPORTANCE OF MODELING BEHAVIOR

"The hope of a secure and livable world lies with disciplined nonconformists who are dedicated to justice, peace and brotherhood." – Dr. Martin Luther King Jr.

Modeling is one way in which behavior is learned. When a person observes the behavior of another and then imitates that behavior, he or she is modeling the behavior. This is sometimes known as observational learning or social learning. Modeling is a kind of vicarious learning in which direct instruction need not occur. Indeed, one may not be aware that another is modeling his or her behavior. Modeling may teach a new behavior, influence the frequency of a previously learned behavior, or increase the frequency of a similar behavior. As it relates to emotional civility, modeling the correct behavior is key to change.

Political modeling of civil behavior (or the modeling of incivility) seems to have the greatest effect on civility in our society. It has been found that seven in 10 Americans (69%) rate the government as uncivil. Regardless of political affiliation, Americans agree that incivility is a major problem today, that it has gotten worse over the past few years and that it is not likely to improve soon. Politicians are most frequently cited as the cause of worsening civility (62%) and the older Americans are the more they blame political leaders. General attitudes toward incivility in government and politics remain largely unchanged from previous years. The vast majority (83%) of Americans believes that politics is becoming increasingly uncivil and that incivility in government is harming our country's future (82%). These attitudes are shared by Americans regardless of political party affiliation. Our nation's political process and the personal lives of Americans are both threatened by political incivility. Nearly seven in 10 Americans (68%) believe that political incivility deters qualified people from going into public service. On a personal level, approximately one-third of Americans report that uncivil expression of political views cost them a friendship, both online (37%) and offline (34%), at a significantly higher rate than in 2012.

It has been hypothesized that political incivility may be approaching the "new normal," and this year's results provide more confirming evidence. Americans still seem resigned to the idea that incivility is just a part of the political process (39%) and that political disagreements between Democrats and Republicans can no longer be discussed civilly (71%). Unfortunately, 80% of Americans believe that our nation's civility problem won't improve until our government leaders act more civilly. Faced with a sort of paradox, American public life may be plagued by incivility for years to come.

The vast majority of Americans agree that civility is important to our democracy (89%), and civility among our elected officials at all levels, including the presidential level, is equally important (92%

and 91%, respectively). When asked about the way members of Congress debate issues facing this country compared to 10 years ago, about seven in 10 (69%) believe they are less civil, and only 8% view Congress as more civil. The impact of incivility on our politics is significant. A majority believes that incivility leads to political gridlock (73%), less political involvement (71%), and fewer people running for public office (61%).

Modeling civility (or incivility) in Politics plays a role at a micro level as well. Americans respond to incivility differently, depending on their political affiliation. Democrats are significantly more likely than Republicans and Independents to have stopped communicating with someone during the past year because they had a different political point of view (50% vs. 38% and 35%, respectively).

When it comes to specific topics Americans avoid discussing for fear the conversation will turn uncivil, Republicans avoid more topics on average than Democrats and Independents (5.0 vs. 4.3 and 4.1, respectively). Politics tops the list of topics Americans, in total, avoid. The top three avoided issues are consistent for Democrats and Republicans: President Trump (first for Democrats, second for Republicans), politics (second for Democrats, first for Republicans) and the border wall with Mexico (third for both Democrats and Republicans). Independents are also most likely to avoid discussing President Trump and politics (tied at first), but also place LGBTQ equality among their top topics to avoid discussing. We have certainly witnessed the highest levels of modeling incivility during the Trump administration, culminating in the attack on the Capitol due to his rhetoric. Just prior to completing this manuscript, a horrific shooting at a spa in Atlanta, Ga rocked our nation. More Asian Americans are battling severe online hate and harassment as rhetoric blaming Chinese people for the coronavirus pandemic has spread on social networks throughout the year. About 17% of Asian Americans said in January they experienced severe online harassment compared with 11% during the same period last year, the largest uptick compared with other groups, according to the Anti-Defamation League (ADL).

The nonprofit (ADL) defines severe online harassment as "stalking, physical threats, swatting, doxing or sustained harassment." About half said they were harassed because of their race. The ADL also found there was a rise in online harassment of African Americans based on their race, which increased from 42% to 59% this year. The ADL has been tracking two other categories of hate, including any online hate and harassment and identity-based online harassment. About 41% of Americans said they experienced online hate and harassment. Americans experienced the most harassment on Facebook followed by Twitter, Instagram and Google-owned YouTube, according to the survey. According to Dr. Tiffany Karalis Noel, a clinical assistant professor and director of doctoral studies in the Department of Learning and Instruction at the University at Buffalo, the "California State University's Center for the Study of Hate and Extremism reported that anti-Asian hate crimes surged by 149% in 2020." Another report indicated nearly 3,800 anti-Asian incidents were recorded between March 19th of 2020 through February 28th of this year. Many report that the surge is coming from xenophobia - that fear of the "unknown." "By tying the names of people, countries, and specific regions and locations to something like a flu or a virus, or something that people are afraid of, then yes, that bullseye and that target is going to perpetuate that fear," according to Karalis Noel. "That fear is going to be exacerbated, and it's going to lead to a lot of these surges that are represented by the data." The fear of the unknown often leads to incivility and uncivil actions, attitudes and responses.

Targets of incivility often punish their offenders. However, emotionally civility understands that vengeance is not appropriate. All too often we underestimate the power and virtue of modeling civility. *You just want us all to be nice*, folks say – as if there is something wrong with just trying to be nice. But civility is about so much more than manners or mood. It is about so much more than politeness or political correctness. Civility is about intentionality and hard work. It takes intentionality and hard work to choose courses of action that are difficult and often unpopular. It takes intentionality and hard work to put the common good above personal agenda, anger, frustration, greed, or fatigue. Civility's payoff, however, is huge. It dramatically effects a kinder world if we commit to civility in the face of civility.

There is no better example of modeling civility than Nelson Mandela. Mr. Mandela, 95, led South Africa's transition from white-minority rule in the 1990s, after 27 years in prison. *Mr.* Mandela was imprisoned in 1962, having been convicted of sabotage and conspiracy to overthrow the white-minority government of South Africa. He remained on a US terror watch list until 2008, and was once described by late British Prime Minister Margaret Thatcher as the leader of a terrorist organization (The African National Congress). But that is not his legacy. After his 1990 release, Mandela worked closely with the South African government to negotiate a peaceful end to apartheid and establish racially inclusive elections.

A hero in life, the choices Nelson Mandela made and the leadership he displayed helped achieve a peace and a future for South Africa that no one had ever even dared to dream, much less act upon. His example and legacy set the standard for statesmanship, selflessness, and civility. How tragic if we only admire him, and do not follow his example. Nelson Mandela left a legacy of civility for us to follow. Nelson Mandela wrote the following that perfectly describes emotional civility: "After I became president, I asked one day some members of my close protection to stroll with me in the city, have lunch at one of its restaurants. We sat in one of the downtown restaurants and all of us asked for some sort of food. After a while, the waiter brought us our requests, I noticed that there is someone sitting in front of my table waiting for food. I told then one of the soldiers: 'Go and ask that person to join us with his food and eat with us.' The soldier went and asked the man so. The man brought up his food and sat by my side as I asked and began to eat. His hands were trembling constantly until everyone had finished their food and the man went. The soldier said to me: 'The man was apparently quite sick. His hands trembled as he ate!' 'No, not at all,' said Mandela.

'This man was the guard of the prison where I was jailed. Often, after the torture I was subjected to, I used to scream and ask for a little water. The very same man used to come every time and urinate on my head instead.' So I found him scared, trembling, expecting me to reciprocate now, at least in the same way, either by torturing him or imprisoning him as I am now the president of the state of South Africa. But this is not my character nor part of my ethics." What an outstanding example of Emotional Civility. How often do we retaliate for much less? Nelson Mandela is an outstanding example of modeling behavior that reflects emotional civility-a civil response in the face of incivility. We as leaders have a duty to reflect that conduct. Another more personal example for me as a model of emotional civility is my Pastor-Bishop Glen A. Staples. A general and giant in church leadership-he walks in great power and humility. Pastoring can sometimes be a very thankless profession. Pastor pray for and often times sacrifice time and money for church members-and get little in return. In fact, sometimes those you help the most are the members that talk about you and turn their backs on you. I have watched Bishop Staples react to incivility with the grace and kindness of Christ. Always exhibiting the fruits of the spirit as outlined in the bible, and always extends grace and forgiveness when many of us would react much differently if faced with similar harsh and hurtful circumstances. We should pay attention close attention to those who model emotional civility and attempt to replicate the behavior in our own lives. We should also remain aware that there is always someone watching. We are under constant scrutiny and close watch by those around us. We should govern ourselves accordingly and think before we speak and act.

CHAPTER EIGHT

CIVILITY IN THE WORKPLACE – LIONS AND KITTENS

"Protect your destiny by vowing to refrain yourself from thinking or speaking whatever it is you aren't willing to embrace it's reality from the universes"— Edmond Mbiaka

I have been blessed to have many exciting and influential positions throughout my career. I was a public defender and Deputy Trial Chief; I was a Professor of Law at Georgetown Law School, Harvard Law School, and Howard Law School; the Senior Deputy for Public Protection and Enforcement at the Attorney General's Office in DC. I walked off a six figure plus job with discussions about me taking over the helm of the Corporation Counsel's Office – what is now the Attorney General's Office. I had the honor of standing with Mayor Anthony Williams in making some of the greatest decisions for the District of Columbia and stood with him in the Emergency Command Center on 9/11. I participated in writing the State of Emergency Legislation for the District that day. I am strong, opinionated, struggle to hold my tongue when I feel I can contribute to a conversation. In 2008 I transitioned to work full time in ministry as the General Counsel and Community

Development Coordinator for the Temple of Praise under the GREAT Bishop Glen A. Staples. It was a move that many criticized and condemned. The day I resigned I was getting a promotion. It was one of the biggest decisions of my life. It was a leap of faith; following the direction of God. Like most faith decisions, it cost me, but that is another book.

When I made the transition from public legal official I was managing hundreds of lawyers and soon to be lawyers; I then walked into a completely new environment. My tone was the tone I had used for over ten years in directing and communication to lawyers and politicians. Managing the staff at the church and CDC was different. Staff complained to Bishop Staples. They said I was mean and that I talked down to them. I was appalled! I was just being efficient and effective. The conversation I had with my Pastor was life changing. He told me in this environment I was a lion in a room full of kittens. When a Lion opens her mouth in a room full of lion cubs the volume, the sound and manner of the lion's voice would not matter. In fact, the lion cubs may run toward the lion. In a room full of kittens, the lion's voice would be overwhelming, threatening, intimidating. Moral of the story: KNOW YOUR ROOM! Knowing your room contributes considerably to emotional civility.

How you communicate is important. I will state this many times in this book. Words matter. Taking the time to formulate a response and understanding your audience is incredibly important to the fight for civility and the promotion of the concept of emotional civility-CIVILITY worldwide! I embrace freedom of speech and I am a fierce advocate of civil rights. However, I understand that self-monitoring of hostile, unnecessary, derogatory, and hateful remarks and a tone reflecting disgust and hate only throws gasoline on an already charge fire of incendiary moments or in many circumstances is the spark that ignites the fire. Commonality and peaceful discourse and resolution is often never accomplished or significantly delayed simply because we did not take the time to think before we speak and choose civility over incivility. This is the process of EC that I am challenging the world to embrace and return to. Studies have shown that it's not just what you say, but how you say it, that effects our relationships and undergirds manner of speech as a hallmark of emotional civility. In fact, this has been confirmed by some well-known research conducted by Dr. Albert Mehrabian. His studies concluded that communication is 7% verbal and 93% non-verbal. A comment directed to you in a sarcastic or critical tone comes across as a negative blow. Yet hearing the same words, delivered in a kind and loving tone, has an entirely different feel. The big communication difference lies in the tone of voice we choose when we communicate with others. Most of us don't pay enough attention to how our tone of voice (as well as the words we use) affects our interactions with others. We so often justify why we are entitled to use a particular tone or, as in my case, often don't even recognize that we are using a certain tone that can be offensive. An aggressive tone can come off attacking and challenging, even if that was not your intention. Indeed, personally this has been one of my biggest personal impediments in communicating.

One of the more concerning workplace trends is the rise in Americans leaving their jobs because of incivility. From 2011 to 2013, there was a 30% increase in Americans reporting they have quit a job because it was an uncivil workplace (20% vs. 26%). People who are more likely than the average American to have quit include those ages 18-34 (34%), parents (32%) and those with a household income under $50K (31%). This willingness to quit a job creates a threat to company reputation and imposes extra costs due to worker turnover. Negative word of mouth and the spread of critical information about a workplace make it difficult for companies to hire top talent and maintain a loyal customer following. Because both current and former employees can help shape a company's reputation, there is a need to maintain a civil workplace.

A large percentage of those surveyed indicated that they had personally experienced incivility at work and in general there was a tone and marked level of uncivility of the workplace. "Since reputation is a company's most competitive asset, workplace incivility cannot be taken for granted. Incivility can negatively impact retention and recruitment not to mention customer service. Ultimately, there's a reputation cost."

(Civility in America: A Nationwide Survey
https://www.webershandwick.com/news/civility - (2010).

I also examined a study regarding the modeling of civility. The aim of the study was to investigate workplace incivility as a social process, examining its components and relationships to both instigated incivility and negative outcomes in the form of well-being, job satisfaction, turnover intentions, and sleeping problems. The different components of incivility that were examined were experienced and witnessed incivility from coworkers as well as supervisors. In addition, the organizational factors, social support, control, and job demands were included in the models. A total of 2,871 (2,058 women and 813 men) employees who were connected to the Swedish Hotel and Restaurant Workers Union completed an online questionnaire. Overall, the results from structural equation modelling indicate that whereas instigated incivility to a large extent was explained by witnessing coworker incivility, negative outcomes were to a high degree explained by experienced supervisor incivility via mediation through perceived low social support, low control, and high job demands. Unexpectedly, the relationships between incivility (experienced coworker and supervisor incivility, as well as witnessed supervisor incivility) and instigated incivility were moderated by perceived high control and high social support. The results highlight the importance of modeling what you expect. Be open about how others perceive you. While the opinions of others don't define you, emotional civility requires a concern about the values that you model. It is important when examining emotional civility that we do not lose time because of ego. When pride has the wheel purpose suffers. Emotional civility requires that we remain teachable and humble. Emotional civility requires that we do not combative when we experience new thoughts and opinions and ideas. We must be flexible to see things and hear things from different perspectives. We can always disagree, but we do not need to be disagreeable in the process.

CHAPTER NINE

MANAGING YOUR EMOTIONS-MONITORING THE VULNERABLE PLACE

If you do not have control over your mouth, you will not have control over your future." — Germany Kent

It is widely known; we make bad decisions based on emotions. If we are scared, upset, sick, or under pressure to perform our emotions can cause us to make huge mistakes. Some that may take years to unravel. If you were honest you can point to times in your life when you made a bad decision or acted out of character because you were in a bad frame of mind. It is our hope that this book reminds you to pause and step back BEFORE you make a bad decision that can cost you. If it has already happened, know that if you fall it does not make you a failure. The best thing you can do it get up, and get up quickly, and try again. Emotional Civility requires you recognize when you are wrong, where you have made your mistakes and learn from them.

One way to maintain a check and reign on your emotions is through mindfulness and intentionality. Taking time to recognize where you are on the emotional spectrum is a key to maintaining emotional civility. One of my favorite practices is the Miracle Morning SAVERS routine. The author, Hal Elrod who has an incredible testimony of survival, developed the concept of SAVERS to help him maintain his emotions with an early morning practice. The acronym stands for: S -Silence A-Affirmations V- Visualization E- Exercise R–Reading S- Scribe. Thousands have found that with this once daily practice the following results occur: puts you in a positive mental state; bolster's confidence; keeps your goals at the top of your mind; increases your energy; kick starts your brain and encourages self-reflection. Finding a strategy that helps ground you in the morning and find peace consistently, and BEFORE you act out emotionally, is key. It can assist you in remaining civil.

Consider becoming part of the Miracle Morning Social Media community. It really helped me at a time where I was hit emotionally with a lot of challenges (death of a loved one-transition in employment-and family matters) simultaneously. It helped me hit the reset button.

It should also be noted that grief is a natural response to loss. It's the emotional suffering you feel when something or someone you love is taken away. Often, the pain of loss can feel overwhelming. You may experience all kinds of difficult and unexpected emotions, from shock or anger to disbelief, guilt, and profound sadness. The pain of grief can also disrupt your physical health, making it difficult to sleep, eat, or even think straight. These are normal reactions to loss – and the more significant the loss, the more intense your grief will be. There is a direct link between grief and emotional civility, and uncivility. When you are grieving you are more likely to act on your emotions because when you are grieving you are often unaware how easily you can say or do the wrong thing in responding to particular emotional stimuli. Coping with the loss of someone or something you love is one of life's biggest challenges. You may associate grieving with the death of a loved one—which is often the cause of the most intense type of grief—but any loss can cause grief, including:

- Divorce or relational break up
- Loss of health
- Losing a job
- Loss of financial stability
- A miscarriage
- Retirement
- Loss of a cherished dream
- A loved one's serious illness
- Loss of a friendship
- Loss of safety and trauma
- Selling the family home
- The incarceration of a child
- A child moving away and going to college

Any one of these situations can cause and emotional reaction. I personally have experienced about four of the occurrences all at the same time. Even subtle losses in life can trigger a sense of grief and trigger emotional uncivility. For example, you might grieve after moving away from home, graduating from college, or changing jobs. Whatever your loss, it's personal to you, so don't feel ashamed about how you feel, or believe that it's somehow only appropriate to grieve for certain things. If the person, animal, relationship, or situation was significant to you, it's normal to grieve the loss you're experiencing. Whatever the cause of your grief, though, there are healthy ways to cope with the pain that, in time, can ease your sadness and help you come to terms with your loss, find new meaning, and eventually move on with your life. During the grieving phase – again – ensuring you are aware of your emotions is key. It is during the grieving phase that we find numerous instances of emotional incivility and we are more apt to respond in a less than civil manner when we are grieving and when we are hurt. It is widely known that hurt people – hurt people. Emotional Intelligence requires that we acknowledge our emotions and emotional civility requires that we respond appropriately regardless of the circumstances.

Grieving is a highly individual experience; there's no right or wrong way to grieve. How you grieve depends on many factors, including your personality and coping style, your life experience, your faith, and how significant the loss was to you. Inevitably, the grieving process takes time. Healing happens gradually; it can't be forced or hurried, and there is no "normal" timetable for grieving. Some people start to feel better in weeks or months. For others, the grieving process is measured in years. Whatever your grief experience, it's important to be patient with yourself and allow the process to naturally unfold. When you are grieving watch your responses and your perception about how you believe people are responding to you.

I certainly can point to each and every moment on this list; and very specific times when I reacted before I processed information and regretted each and every decision or response. As I grieved my parent's death, and I can pinpoint instances of emotional incivility where I said and did something in response to a negative interaction during my grieving process that I regretted. My son left for college, my divorce, loss of a home after divorce, all put me in an emotional state where I found myself reacting in ways that went against my values. I practiced emotional incivility and most of the time I was not aware of it. Despite making some very wrong turns, and bad decisions professionally, God has been merciful, and full of grace. When evaluating communication from the lens of emotional civility, it is important for you to be kind to yourself and others who are traveling in the same direction. It is hard to tell another person how to feel if we have never walked in their shoes. So be careful how you communicate. Just remember when dealing with a person who is weary – don't add criticism or rage to their brokenness. There are many ways to calm a negative energy without suppressing or fighting it. You recognize it, you smile at it, and you invite something nicer to come up and replace it. You read some inspiring words, you listen to a piece of beautiful music, you go somewhere in nature, or you do some walking and mediation. This is how you handle it. This is how you remain emotionally civil. I truly believe that we are not the mistakes we make, and we are afforded opportunities to learn from our mistakes and we become better as a result. Knowing how you are emotionally processing a loss or processing stress can help prevent a negative response to negative stimuli. When experiencing loss or when we are under stress we can misinterpret information or act out from our place of grief. We must be careful – one bad reaction can cost us our livelihood. On the other hand, let us be forgiving of those who we know are experiencing challenges. Emotional Civility teaches us to manage how we react to stimuli, particularly at a time when we are most vulnerable emotionally- whether on the giving end or the receiving end. The impetus for this book is not just that I did everything right but my desire to help prevent others from making the same mistake or console those who may think that their last uncivil response was death to their opportunity and their last chance. If you are reading this book, I offer you hope. It is because you care and because you want to do better and be better that you will achieve what you believe.

CHAPTER TEN

SOCIAL MEDIA AND ITS IMPACT ON SOCIAL CIVILITY

Civility remains a "major" problem in America—and social media is only making it worse. – Richard Carufe

3.5 billion out of the 7.5 billion people in the world use social media daily. Those 3.5 billion people rely on social media for everything from news, to validation, positive or negative outlets, and most of all to hide behind a screen. A statistic states that out of those 3.5 billion people "the average person spends nearly 2 hours a day which amounts to 5 years and 4 months of their lifetime." It's a shame to think that these are 5 years and 4 months we could never get back, but even more shameful to those who use this time to hurt others. As adults, we do still feel a burn or sting when someone insults us but compared to the minds of young children and teenagers we are better equipped. During our adolescent years, our minds are very much premature and easily manipulated because they are learning what is supposed to be normal as well as developing our identities. "5.7 million children under the age of 11 have accounts on Facebook, Instagram, and Snapchat – all of which have age restrictions that are intended to keep children from using them." 5.7 million children under the age of 11 are exposed to social media sites that are intended for adults. Unknowingly being exposed to things that are inappropriate and filled with insensitive and endangering content have created an environment where we have become normalized to insensitivity. Instead of exploring interests and developing identities through real life experiences, social media users become reliant on social media to map out how they live. It is fantasy not reality. Their emotions are based on this fantasy and when hit with reality, they act out emotionally.

The following are social media statistics among children:

- The number of sexual assault cases involving children has increased by 300% in the past year

- 88% of teens have seen someone be mean or cruel to another person on social media

- 29% of internet sex crime relationships were initiated on a social networking site

- 55% of parents say their 12-year-old was on Facebook and 76% said they helped their child gain access

- 8% were involved in a physical fight with someone else because of something posted on a social networking site

- 67% of teens say they know how to hide what they do online from their parents

- 55% of teens have given out personal information to someone they don't know including photos and physical descriptions

- Among 9-17-year-olds, more time is spent on social media than tv

- 71% of 9-17-year-olds visit these sites weekly

- 29% have been stalked or contacted by a stranger or someone they don't know

- 24% have had private photos and information made public without their permission Besides the many alarming statistics reflecting the physical danger of social media, the ultimate effect on our brains is just as potent. Becoming emotionally civil cannot be achieved if we base our decisions and actions on what social media has allowed us to do. Emotional civility stems from real-life experiences that strengthen our ability to be productive through any tough situation or adversity. If we do not work our brains to find answers for ourselves instead of relying on others and the media, we will truly never find ourselves nor ultimately live. Social media, instead of empowering, has become an escape from reality and has put a majority of us on the ignorant side of things- particularly as it relates to processing our emotions.

Online bullying – or "cyberbullying" – continues to be of great concern to our press towards a more civil society and more civil interactions. As more Americans blame the Internet for rising incivility, more Americans report that cyberbullying is getting worse. Significantly more people believe cyberbullying in society is getting worse, and concern over children being cyberbullied is at its highest level since we began our study in 2010. It is widely known that incivility triggers changes in online behavior. Because of the lack of civility in behavior or tone of conversation, nearly half of

Emotional Civility

Americans (48%) have defriended, blocked, or hidden someone online, nearly four in 10 have flagged or reported a comment or post as inappropriate (39%) or have stopped going to an online site because it made them uncomfortable (36%). One-third (33%) opted out of an online discussion altogether. Slightly fewer (30%) have dropped out of an uncivil fan club or online community.

These changes in online behavior may have both positive and negative implications. On the one hand, Americans may be taking a stand against incivility by refusing to deal with inappropriate online behavior and declining to visit sites where they encounter incivility. But these actions also suggest that people who may have more balanced viewpoints are driven out of conversations and from sites they would otherwise take part in. Either way, Americans are developing coping mechanisms to deal with their online experiences of rude and uncivil discourse.

It is not surprising that more people are experiencing uncivil behavior online than in-person given our growing use of and reliance on the Internet. Contributing heavily to the cause of online incivility is social media, with 63% of Americans saying that, in their experience, the impact of social media on civility has been more negative than positive. Only nine percent say it has been more positive than negative. Negativity decidedly outweighs positivity by large margins regardless of gender or generation. Even within the generation that is native to social media — Generation Z (who in our study are 16–21 years old) — a massive gap emerges of nearly 4:1 between those who say social media's effect has been more negative than positive vs. more positive than negative (56% vs. 15%, respectively). More than one-half of Americans (54%) expect the general tone and level of civility in the country to decline even further during the next few years. Among this group, 57% believe that the Internet and/or social media are to blame – a factor that tops a list of 19 possible choices measured this year.

Most recently, Donald Trump's use of social media attracted worldwide attention. Prior to his social media bans in 2021, he frequently used Twitter and other social media platforms to make comments about other politicians, celebrities, private citizens, and daily news. From his official declaration of candidacy in June 2015 through the four years of his presidency, he tweeted over 34,000 times. Since early in his presidency, his tweets have been considered official statements made by the president of the United States. On January 6, 2021, after the storming of the United States Capitol while Congress was certifying the vote in favor of president-elect Joe Biden, Twitter warned Trump not to incite further violence. According to Twitter, Trump did not comply, and on January 8, Twitter permanently suspended his @realDonaldTrump handle, followed by the official account of his campaign shortly thereafter. Additionally, Facebook blocked and later banned Trump from all of its platforms indefinitely, at least until his presidential term ends.

Other social media companies have since restricted or blocked his accounts.

One of the most heavily debated issues on civility is whether social media holds a remedial responsibility given its role as a top driver of incivility. Another question is whether social media could also be used to help turn the tide. Nearly four in 10 Americans (38%) say they would be willing to personally engage with social media to improve civility by taking at least one of the following actions:

- Posting more positive things on social media about things they see happening (23%)

- Flagging information shared on social media that is uncivil (20%)

- Publicly sharing or posting stories, photos or videos about people who act uncivilly (13%)

The public also wants social media companies to help mitigate the uncivil behavior their platforms are perceived to be encouraging. Nearly six in 10 Americans (57%) are of the opinion that social media companies should take a larger role in helping improve the level of civility in our nation. While this isn't as high as the responsibility Americans believe elected officials should take – the top-ranked institution for taking on a larger role at 64% -- it is on par with the responsibility expected from state and local governments (57%). As we move toward a more civil society – globally- we all should take our responsibility toward social media use much more seriously. In this new emotional civility paradigm- thoughtful use of social media is critical.

CHAPTER ELEVEN

EXTERNAL SOURCES – SILENCING THE NOISE WHICH DRIVES US AWAY FROM CIVILITY

"Often times God wants us to sit before Him in quietness. He doesn't want us to do all the talking. "In quiet and confidence will be your strength." — Charles Stanley

Silence. Some of us welcome it. For others, the thought of sitting in silence is enough to make their skin crawl. Silence offers opportunities for self-reflection and daydreaming, which activates multiple parts of the brain. It gives us time to turn down the inner noise and increase awareness of what matters most. And it cultivates mindfulness — recognition and appreciation of the present moment.

We live in a day where 'demonstrations' taking the form of protests and marches fill our screens, and uncivil statements made by news anchors, colleagues, and neighbors fill our ears. With a rapidly growing lack of respect for people's freedom to hold their own beliefs without scorn or reproach from someone they know, Emotional Civility is important. In a time where news stations have become all-out war zones and not even family reunions are safe spaces, it is very easy to lose sight of optimism. Many people look at a time like this and say, "What could possibly be worse?" You have a once "trusted" friend who, after an election, has become your greatest "enemy" and critic. People are afraid to say whom they voted for, fearing that someone in their midst will see their beliefs as the work of pure evil. With so much noise surrounding us from everywhere-where can we turn to ground ourselves so that we can ensure an emotionally civil response? What can we do to help ensure that we act with Emotional Civility and are not affected by everything going on around us in a negative way?

Taking a break from social media allows us to silence society's voices and get in tune with our own voice, emotions, and perspectives. Social media is the constant comparison, insecurity, and nosiness of trying to stay in the know, be liked, show who we like and don't like, prominent disruption of peace. Peace, silence, and a moment to reflect helps us to be in tune with our own emotions so when the negative stimuli hit, we are prepared to respond.

In the moments when we find complete fulfillment from social media, life is good. But to be real, for most of us, our relationships with these apps aren't always so perfect. On one hand, social media is convenient. It allows us to stay in touch, keep up with the news and trends and offers the chance to be exposed to new art and ideas. At the same time, it sometimes has its ways of leaving us feeling more disconnected.

For many- while they love staying up to date on how my friends and family are doing and celebrating snapshot moments in their lives, I'll admit that my interaction with social media apps tends to be more automated than that. At the end of a long day, scrolling through

Facebook and Instagram offers an alluring release — even if the content is just white noise.

In the 2020 documentary "The Social Dilemma," viewers heard first-hand from leaders in Silicon Valley about the dark side of social media and how it's used to keep us hooked. To quote the film's Edward Tufte, professor emeritus at Yale University, "There are only two industries that call their customers 'users': illegal drugs and software." Examining a study of Biopsychology, Cognition, and Neuroscience at the University of Michigan I became much more interested in documentaries like this, specifically how they are connected with the biological and physiological processes of the brain.

Like with any kind of addiction, such as cocaine or gambling, habitual social media use keeps us neurologically hooked by working on what is called our dopaminergic pathways. Dopamine, a feel-good chemical in the brain, floods our synapses every time we use social media habitually. Through a process known as long-term potentiation, the neural pathways involved in addiction become stronger with every click, like paths through the woods that harden as more travelers walk across them. The more we activate these pathways by repeatedly performing similar actions or forming dependent behaviors, the stronger they become and the harder it is to quit. In essence, habitual use of a substance or behavior leads to a type of hard wiring that keeps us doing what feels good, even if it affects us in negative ways. Emotional Civility requires that we take a break.

So how do you break the cycle? While you could decide to just use social media less, realistically, that may not work for everyone. If you've ever tried to quit something, like cutting out sugar from your diet or quitting nicotine, you may have noticed that even after long periods of meeting your goals, it's easy to fall back into old habits.

If the "just use less" approach isn't working for you, next time you find yourself using social media to fulfill your dopamine needs, a secondary strategy you could try is engaging with mindfulness.

What is mindfulness? The University of Michigan Health Service, defines it as "the practice of being present and deliberately aware of our inner thoughts, feelings and surroundings. Mindfulness meditation has been shown to reduce stress, improve sleep, and improve cognitive functioning."

As you give yourself space to breathe, it is important bring some intentionality and gratitude into your practice. Similar to how you might pray before a meal, say thank you to what you're about to consume. Take a moment to visualize the energy and the people you're about to connect with. Notice what feelings come up. You may find that this lends itself to forming deeper connections whether online or in person. Your time is valuable; don't waste it on what doesn't add value.

By practicing mindfulness with your social media consumption, you allow yourself to move from habitual behavior to a place of mindful reflection that nourishes your relationships, your community, and your soul. Life is short, fill your feed with what matters to you. Break the noise so that you can have a moment to breathe and pray and take in positivity and not be bogged down by negativity. You are less likely to respond emotionally than if you are consistently confronted with the negatively from social media, TV, news and other outside influences. Emotional civility requires that you take a break from the constant noise that bombards us everyday to ensure that our responses are consistent and emotionally appropriate.

CHAPTER TWELVE

RELATIONSHIPS AND CIVILITY

"The meeting of two personalities is like the contact of two chemical substances: if there is any reaction, both are transformed." — Carl Gustav Jung

Over the last couple of decades, sociologists, commentators, public officials and other observers have been telling us that civility and civil communication is fast disappearing from our society.

Countless books, articles and reports are being churned out addressing what many refer to as our "rudeness epidemic." Surveys conducted around the globe report that discourteous behavior, vulgar language, and displays of anger are at all-time highs – even in marriages and personal relationships. The COVID pandemic and the effect of quarantine has seen a rise in the instances of domestic violence. On the surface, most displays of callousness may seem innocuous. But even these relatively minor infractions matter, particularly as it relates to the health of relationships. The attitudes that are at the root of everyday incidents of incivility can turn into the bigger episodes we hear about on the news – domestic assaults and, even worse, domestic homicide.

Civility is essential for stable, strong, and harmonious relationships. When individuals show concern for each other, not only do their relationships become stronger, society as a whole functions better. To be civil is to behave in a way that takes into account the well-being of others – to show courtesy, concern and regard. When civility breaks down, civilization begins to fracture. Johns' Hopkins professor P.M. Forni warns in his 2008 best seller, The Civility Solution, that incivility often escalates into violence. Another trend is our society's ever-increasing focus on me. While human beings have always had a tendency to think about themselves first and foremost, numerous studies suggest that, as a culture, we are becoming more self-absorbed than ever. The signs are everywhere.

Just look at all the self-promotion on social media sites, the boom in cosmetic surgery and the increasing materialism. In the book, The Civility Solution, Forni writes that when "self" is king, "we are not inclined to be considerate and kind. Furthermore, when life does not grant us the privileges, we expect given the high opinion we have of ourselves, frustration and anger are likely to result, with the attending abuse of innocent bystanders." Just over the last month, I have had some very interesting interactions with potential business partners that made me very uncomfortable and made me work hard to apply my own EC paradigm. After working on a project for months, there was a change in direction that I did not feel was handled appropriately. My response, while not uncivil, remained professional. I was incredibly disappointed, and felt betrayed and that the colleagues were not acting with transparency or honestly. I spoke my truth -and it was not received well. These are the difficult times and difficult choices for emotionally civility. Sometime when you speak your mind- you are confronted and challenged for speaking your truth. This again is where the challenge lies in the discussion about civility. Sometimes just stating your truth is seen as uncivil and taken as an attack. Do we speak up or do we remain silent? Emotional civility does not mean that we remain silent! It means we take time to process the emotion that gives rise to the thought that we are about to articulate. Some of the questions we must sit with before responding are: Is it OUR truth or THE truth? Are we overreacting? How do we communicate the concerns so that they are received productively? Emotional Civility requires that pause, that breath, that tear, that moment of rest and reflection. In re-evaluating my own situation, I would have waited and prayed before I spoke my truth. The delay, I believe would have made a difference in building the business relationship. EC takes constant work to get it right.

Some of the blame for incidents of emotional civility in personal relationships can also be attributed to people working longer hours, leading busier lives and, in general, being under more stress. All this pressure and anxiety can make us less tolerant of others. In his 2002 book, Choosing Civility, Forni writes: "A stressed, fatigued, or distressed person is less inclined to be patient and tolerant, to think before acting, and to be aware of the needs of others. Thus such a person is more likely to be rude." Rudeness is synonymous with uncivility. This rudeness often plays out not just in public settings but in private settings – in marriages; in relationships between siblings; and between parents and children. The incidents of elder abuse have also increased during the pandemic as stress, fatigue, and mental health issues during the pandemic have surfaced. The need to practice emotional civility privately as well as publicly is clear now more than ever. Incivility often becomes a self-perpetuating cycle: When we're rude with others, we tend to feel more stress, which leads to more rudeness, and then we're more stressed and on and on. In fact, Civility is often the first things to disappear when a marriage becomes distressed, often never to return. Reintroducing civility and good will into a marriage can have a powerful impact on a couple's marital satisfaction. It allows couples to improve their communication and it introduces a far more positive and mutually caring tone into the home. It profits nothing if we focus on maintaining civil interactions publicly and do nothing to work on our private interaction. We must strive to practice emotional civility when its hard. Sometimes we take our loved ones and those closest to us for granted and lash out at those we are most connected with. Emotional Civility requires that we remember the old adage - Civility/charity starts at home.

CHAPTER THIRTEEN

SCHOOLS AND YOUTH AND CIVILITY

"Times like these always reveal that the veil of civility is thinner than we thought... but that the hearts of good people are greater than we imagined." — Steve Maraboli

B ecause youth are still developing in so many critical ways, it's vital that they learn empathy and critical thinking while they're young. When adults are sending them mixed messages through words or actions, it's hard for youth to develop those important emotional civility skills. We must teach children that civility isn't setting aside truth for the sake of unity; it's showing respect for another human being made in God's image.

The issue, of course, isn't just our words. When we make flippant statements about other people, we reveal what we truly think of them. Right now, there's so much disagreement in our families, churches, and communities about COVID-19, masks, racial injustice, politics, education – you name it. And disagreement is normal. But there has to be a more civil way to disagree with one another and to teach our kids to disagree. After all, our children are growing up in a society that will frequently disagree with their beliefs. How can we equip them to be winsome and humble while also being firm and steadfast? Emotional Civility requires us to teach principles of civility and to teach our youth how to manage their emotions. Civility needs to be taught in school again. The paradigm of emotional civility, I believe should be a key introduction to the curriculum of every school (elementary through high school).

Numerous studies report that parents were significantly more likely to report that their children experienced incivility in schools (62% vs. 50% and 51%). One-third of parents (32%) also say that their children experience incivility in their neighborhood.

Significantly more parents this year report transferring a child to a different school because they were treated uncivilly, either online or off. With children experiencing incivility in their neighborhoods, at school and online, it is likely that incivility in the community as a whole moved a parent to transfer their children. We must be intentional about how our children are taking cues from us and then causing incivility to break out in our schools, and on our playgrounds. I was led to write this book is to remind us – the adults in the room – to remember the impact of our behavior on our children. They overhear the comments, they see how we treat someone that looks different from us, they see how we respond to the cashier in the grocery store who is not moving fast enough – they see the behavior. If our world is going to get better, it starts with us. We must teach civility early. If it doesn't start at home, we must get it in our schools. We must shift our culture. We must honor and replicate the work of Cassandra Dahnke and Tomas Spath, the Founders of the Institute for Civility in Government. Ms. Dahnke and Mr. Spath for years have been investing in the lives of our youth, by teaching civility in elementary, middle, and high schools. Dr. Bertie Simmons literally turned around the lives of hundreds of young people and their families. For 58 years Bertie Simmons, Ed.D. was a dedicated educator in the Houston Independent School District (HISD). The first of Simmons' seemingly countless honors came in 1965, when she was named the HISD Teacher of the Year. During her career in HISD, she served as Assistant Superintendent, District Superintendent, Associate Superintendent, and Executive Director. After retiring in 1995, she returned to the district in 2000 to serve as the principal of Furr High School for 17 years. She is widely regarded for being instrumental in the effort to revitalize the school and create transformational opportunities for some of Houston's most disadvantaged students. Furr was one of only three schools in the nation identified to receive the College Board Inspiration Award in 2011. During her tenure at Furr she received notable professional recognitions that include HEB's Best High School Principal in Texas award in 2011 and KHOU's Schools Now Spirit of Texas award. Known as a visionary and a change agent who can bring out the best in her students, the high-energy educator arrived at Furr High School at 6:30 a.m. each school day. She maintained that upbeat and infectious attitude to reach and inspire her teachers and students with her passion, knowledge, dedication, and maybe even the occasional rap song or two. This is modeling civility in our schools by school leadership.

There are many examples throughout our communities of leaders of civility in and for our school systems. My beloved sorority – Delta Sigma Theta-is renowned for community service and scholarship support. Sorority and Fraternities in the Divine Nine are often trailblazers for working with schools and supporting and training youth to be leaders. The Links Incorporated, an organization with whom my mother was a platinum member, whose members are dedicated to the racial and social uplift of people of African descent through charitable work are leaders of civility for youth. The Links have more than eleven thousand members in over two hundred seventy-five chapters in the United States, Germany, the Bahamas, and South Africa have that contributed over twenty million dollars and donated thousands of service hours to various causes for community improvement for nearly fifty years. Educators Margaret Roselle Hawkins and Sarah Strickland Scott conceptualized a club that would link friends in service and established The Links in Philadelphia, Pennsylvania in 1946. The women were deeply concerned with the plight of Negroes in America and their horrific treatment in a racist society. The condition of the masses of Negroes during this period was abysmal due to social inequality in education, employment, and civil rights in the United States. The Links focus on combating the social ills plaguing their communities. Many notable African-American women including my mother Jacquelyn Bowie Styles have held membership in this organization including Drs. Sadie Alexander, Helen Gray Edmonds, Betty Shabazz, Johnetta Cole and Ms. Coretta Scott King. One of their main areas of charitable giving is in the area of scholarship for youth. Civility in our schools and for our youth is a key goal for many African American civic organizations. As we gain success, giving back and teaching civility is our responsibility on all academic levels.

This book is only my first step to introduce the paradigm of emotional civility into the world. My commitment to EC will be to follow-up these manuscript with workbooks to help us all navigate the challenges of interacting with emotional civility. I am also working on curricula for elementary, middle, and high schools and universities to begin to teach and re-introduce civility into public education.

CHAPTER FOURTEEN

HINDSIGHT VS. FORESIGHT

"Civility also requires relearning how to disagree without being disagreeable... surely you can question my policies without questioning my faith." — Barack Obama

Although Americans express deep concern about the state of civility in our country, we also find that many are hopeful about the outlook for our public discourse. However, many Americans also experience hindsight bias. Hindsight bias also known as the knew-it-all-along phenomenon or creeping determinism, is the common tendency for people to perceive past events as having been more predictable than they actually were. People often believe that after an event has occurred, they would have predicted or perhaps even would have known with a high degree of certainty what the outcome of the event would have been before the event occurred. Hindsight bias may cause distortions of memories of what was known or believed before an event occurred, and is a significant source of overconfidence regarding an individual's ability to predict the outcomes of future events. Hindsight bias can be a significant cause of emotional incivility. Again quoting Weber an Shandwick, nearly nine in 10 persons believe it is possible for people to disagree in a civil way, and 60%

express hope about the future of civility. In the same nationwide survey among those who expect civility to get better (17% of those surveyed), the average American is perceived as the top driver of improved civility (42% say average Americans are improving overall civility). Similarly, average Americans are among the lowest drivers of incivility when respondents are asked to choose what is causing the nation's civility erosion; 20% say average Americans are making civility worse, far lower than the top factor of social media and the Internet at 57%.

(Civility in America: A Nationwide Survey https://www.webershandwick.com/news/civility - (2010).

Americans are also willing to take personal responsibility to improve civility in our nation. The vast majority, 88%, selected in the same survey reveal that there is at least one action they would be willing to take to improve civility. Topping the list are: making an effort to be civil when treated uncivilly (46%); encouraging family, friends and coworkers to be civil (45%); and voting for political leaders who behave in a civil way (43%).

Importantly, a significant 62% of Americans say that if an organization existed to make it easier to support civility or get involved, they would be likely to participate or support it. The same survey identified a segment of the population,16%, who would be very likely to participate in this type of organization and dubbed them Civility Advocates (Civility in America: A Nationwide Survey).

Compared to the average American, Civility Advocates are more likely to be:

- Gen Zs and Millennials

- Parents of kids under 18 years old

- African American or black

- From the Midwest, and less likely to be from the West

- Urban, and less likely to live in suburban areas

Civility Advocates have experienced more incivility compared to the average American. They are more likely to have been the victim of incivility both online and in-person.

Civility Advocates are action takers. When confronted with uncivil behavior, they are more likely than average to respond, including politely defending themselves (46% vs. 27%, respectively), filing a complaint or report (21% vs. 10%), telling friends on social media (19% vs. 9%), and the more passive response of removing themselves from the situation (53% vs. 47%). Civility Advocates have a positive outlook. Civility Advocates are much more likely than other Americans to be very hopeful about the future of civility in the U.S. (42% vs. 17%, respectively). Another 34% are somewhat hopeful. One reason Civility Advocates may be interested in an organization to support civility is that they are strong proponents of community and nonprofit organizations working toward solutions for the nation's incivility crisis. Seven in 10 Civility Advocates (69%) would like community and nonprofits to play a larger role in helping improve civility vs. 42% of average Americans. See (Civility in America: A Nationwide Survey). As I advance the importance of Emotional Civility as a standard of global success, there is a need to develop a generation of Civility Advocates who understand and appreciate the need for emotionally civil responses and to fight against hindsight bias in formulating responses.

THE COST OF "BEING REAL"

Again, citing Cassandra Dahnke and Tomas Spath: Civility is claiming and caring for one's identity, needs and beliefs without degrading someone else's in the process. The First Amendment **to** the U.S. Constitution protects the freedom of speech, religion, and the press. It also protects the right to peaceful protest and to petition the government. Those who act with incivility often hide boldly behind the First Amendment right to free speech by stating that, "There's no exception for hate speech under the First Amendment's protection for freedom of expression." However, it should be noted that if speech is direct, personal, and truly threatening or violently provocative – that speech is not protected. In 1942, the Supreme Court said that the First Amendment doesn't protect "fighting words," or statements that "by their very utterance inflict injury or tend to incite an immediate breach of the peace" (*Chaplinsky v. New Hampshire*, 315 U.S. 568 (1942)). In later decisions, the Court narrowed this exception by honing in on the second part of the definition: direct, personal insults that are so offensive they're likely to provoke their specific target to respond immediately with violence. The Court has also said that laws can't prohibit only some types of fighting words, like those based on racial bias (*R.A.V. v. City of St. Paul,* 505 U.S. 377 (1992)). Courts have generally found that the First Amendment protects speech if it causes only emotional injury, no matter how offensive it is.

But let's go beyond the legalities and look at the impact on community, relationship, and society. Words can hurt. Rhetoric can hurt. We have often heard individuals make the statement, "I'm just being real". "I'm just being honest" when that individual says something at the expense of someone else's feelings. We see individuals trying over and over again to advance their beliefs at the expense of others. Incendiary rhetoric has seeped into presidential politics and went on steroids during the Trump era. Trump's poor word choices often led to ambiguity, disagreements, and confusion on whether he actually meant whatever he said. Politician George Orwell in his essay *Politics and the English Language* has warned against bad English. One must always keep that essay in mind when there is confusion that arises from what someone means. Donald Trump was renowned during his candidacy and presidency for personal attacks and name calling. Many have said that this type of speech exhibited an "alarming willingness to fascist themes and styles." Most infamously, he retweeted and endorsed a quotation from Benito Mussolini, and when confronted about it, said "What difference does it make?" Benito Amilcare Andrea Mussolini was an Italian politician and journalist who founded and led the National Fascist Party. He was Prime Minister of Italy and successfully implemented a Fascist coup d'état in 1922. He was a dictator and founder of the fascist movement and inspired other totalitarian rulers such as Adolf Hitler. Trump frequently makes use of a wide range of logical fallacies. That is the difference, and Trump's words have concerned the world because of what they represent. People know how dangerous words are.

Analytically, Trump's rhetoric is twice as extreme as every US President from Herbert Hoover through Barak Obama. Using extreme language is a method to circumvent or overwhelm reason according to Yale philosopher Jason Stanley who wrote "How Fascism Works." Regardless of whether Trump's policies are fascistic, Trump's rhetoric *is* fascistic and is comparable to the rhetoric of Joseph Goebbles. Extreme rhetoric, including vague and incoherent language, has consequences. In general, Trump's rallies have inspired, or outright incited, an uptick in violence from his supporters all over the nation, including from his own security guards and campaign staffers. Protesters and journalists are often the intended targets. Even when there's no violence, he expresses disappointment at the peace. It's gotten so bad, Trump actually entertained political assassination of Hillary Clinton to keep her from appointing Supreme Court Justices, prompting the Secret Service to host a private meeting with him over his remarks.

From this perspective, the former president's words function as a conduit from his head to everyone listening. With the former president, we have all become accustomed to the concept of misinformation, whereby we recognize that intentionally false or misleading information is transmitted to the listener, and how it's had a devastating impact during the COVID-19 pandemic.

The transmission model of communications describes the technical movement of a signal over a channel and across a distance. But this is not an accurate description of presidential rhetoric. Too often we think that the complex, human task of communication is the same as the technical process of transmission.

What many call the "rhetorical model of communication" suggests is that words have impact, and that meaning is an outcome of the effects words produce. About 2,400 years ago, Gorgias, the famous sophist and democratic theorist, argued that words had a similar effect as drugs on the body. Athenians would speak to the wounds of the soldiers in battles in hopes that their words would heal. So instead of asking whether a president's rhetoric is true or false, instead of trying to interpret the information presented in order to receive an accurate sense of what Trump is really saying, we ought to start asking: What effect do the president's words have on us? For example, what is the impact of his anti-mask mockery on his followers and on public health efforts to keep citizens safe? Parsing the information transmitted by a president, determining whether it's true or false or what's really going on, is an ineffective way to understand what Trump's words actually achieve. It doesn't matter whether the information he transmits is accurate or inaccurate, and we make a mistake when we focus too much on accuracy and inaccuracy. What is the effect of his words on the listeners?

Trump's words are aimed at producing strong reactions. When he mocks mask-wearing, he knows that he'll evoke a strong reaction from both the media and his followers, and he doesn't seem to care about the accuracy of the information he's transmitting. He knows that elections are not won or lost on policy ideas or rational voters making informed choices. They are won or lost on the basis of the effects produced by the candidate's words according to Robert Danisch, an Associate Professor and Communications & Chair of Department of Communication Arts at the University of Waterloo, who has taught rhetoric and communication classes for 20 years. He has been telling his students to pay more attention to the effects their words have on others and not the information they wish to convey. In an article, "The Conversation Under a Creative Commons License" Professor Danisch notes that Trump has surely mastered that lesson of using words. He notes that the Trump speaks with the intent of producing the strongest possible impact and cares not at all about the information transmitted. There is no mistaking the intended effects of this president's rhetoric. He aims to create feelings of resentment, distrust, and suspicion. Mapping the world in terms of "us" and "them" creates conflict (and is perhaps the cornerstone of fascist rhetoric). Words can create conflict with those we resent, and words can cause distrust that drives attention. This is the ethos of the entertainment industry, reality television and thousands of years of theatre. Trump – a reality television star – used words from his experience. Making us feel uncertain, anxious, fearful, this is what Trump's words do, regardless of the information they transmit.

Words matter, words empower, words create. We must choose them wisely. Emotional Civility requires that you intentionally understand and are conscious of the effect your words have on others. The more power you have or position you have – the more conscious you must be about their effect.

Research shows that the messages people consume affect their behaviors in three ways: First, when a person encounters a message that advocates a behavior, that person is likely to believe that the behavior will have positive results. This is particularly true if the speaker of that message is liked or trusted by the target of the message.

Second, when these messages communicate positive beliefs or attitudes about our behavior – as when our friends told us that smoking was "cool" when we were teenagers – message targets come to believe that those they care about would approve of their engaging in the behavior or would engage in the behavior themselves.

Finally, when messages contain language that target's the ability to perform a behavior, as when a president tells raucous supporters that they have the power to overturn an election, they develop the belief that they can actually do what is said. That is what we witnessed at the Capitol.

In the weeks following the election, allies of Trump, only reinforced these beliefs among Trump supporters by perpetuating his lies. With these beliefs and attitudes in place, Trump's January 6th speech outside the White House served as a key accelerant to the attack by sparking the raucous crowd to action. In his pre-attack speech, Trump said that he and his followers should "fight like hell against bad people." He said that they would "walk down Pennsylvania Avenue" to give Republican legislators the boldness they need to "take back the country." He said that "this is a time for strength" and that the crowd was beholden to "very different rules" than would normally be called for. Less than two hours after these words were spoken, violent insurrectionists breached the Capitol.

In the case of Donald Trump, the relationship between words and actions is patently clear. There has never been a more scientifically valid case for incitement. Decades of research have demonstrated that language affects our behaviors – words have consequences. And when those words champion aggression, make violence acceptable and embolden audiences to action, incidents like the insurrection at the Capitol are the result.

Senators, acting in the impeachment trial of former President Donald Trump had to decide whether to convict the former president for inciting a deadly, violent insurrection at the Capitol building on Jan. 6. A majority of House members, including 10 Republicans, took the first step in the two-step impeachment process. They voted to impeach Trump for "incitement of insurrection." Their resolution stated that he "willfully made statements that, in context, encourage – and foreseeably resulted in – lawless action at the Capitol, such as: 'if you don't fight like hell, you're not going to have a country anymore.'"

Emotional Civility

Impeachment proceedings that consider incitement to insurrection are rare in American history. Yet dozens of legislators – including some Republicans – made clear that Trump's actions and words leading up to the Jan. 6 attack on the Capitol contributed to an attempted insurrection against American democracy itself. Such claims against Trump are complicated. Rather than wage direct war against sitting U.S. representatives, Trump is accused of using language to motivate others to do so. Some have countered that the connection between President Trump's words and the violence of Jan. 6 is too tenuous, too abstract, too indirect to be considered viable.

However, decades of research on social influence, persuasion and psychology show that the messages that people encounter heavily influence their decisions to engage in certain behaviors. We know that Trump was acquitted in the Senate. In reality, I do not think that they acquitted Trump because they thought he was innocent. I believe that the Republican Senators were fearful of the standard that would be set if they convicted Trump based on speech. That is why this book is so important and the reminder of operating with Emotional Civility is so important. If we would take the time to choose the right works, not act out of emotion, monitor our conduct, we would not have to worry about situations like this. We can disagree and condemn thoughts that are different from ours without being disagreeable or invoking and stoking violence.

CHAPTER FIFTEEN

THE RESPONSIBITY OF LEADERSHIP AND CIVIILTY

"When people say things that we find offensive, civic charity asks that we resist the urge to attribute to immorality or prejudice views that can be equally well explained by other motives" — Michael Austin

Observational learning theory suggests that when leaders and those held in high esteem in our culture behave in uncivil ways their behavior is modeled and repeated by others. Ethical, principled, collaborative, and trustworthy leaders make a significant contribution to our society and our world. Similarly, unethical, unprincipled, rude, and untrustworthy leaders can tear down the fabric of our country and relationships globally.

A prime example of how uncivil speech and incivility can gravely affect how we communicate in our society is the behavior and conduct of the 45th President of the United States- Donald Trump. Donald Trump's rhetoric changed the way hundreds of children are harassed in American classrooms. Since Trump's rise to the nation's highest office, his inflammatory language — often condemned as racist and xenophobic — has seeped into schools across America. A

Emotional Civility

Washington Post review of 28,000 news stories found Many bullies now target other children differently than they used to, with kids as young as 6 mimicking the president's insults and the cruel way he delivers them. Trump's words, those chanted by his followers at campaign rallies, and even his last name have been wielded by students and school staff members to harass children more than 300 times since the start of 2016. This same report found that at least three-quarters of the attacks were directed at kids who are Hispanic, black, or Muslim according to the analysis. Students have also been victimized because they support the president — more than 45 times during the same period.

Although many hateful episodes garnered coverage just after the election, The Post found that Trump-connected persecution of children has never stopped. Even without the huge total from November 2016, an average of nearly two incidents per school week have been publicly reported over the past four years. Still, because so much of the bullying never appears in the news, The Post's figure represents a small fraction of the actual total. It also doesn't include the thousands of slurs, swastikas, and racial epithets that aren't directly linked to Trump but that the president's detractors argue his behavior has exacerbated.

"It's gotten way worse since Trump got elected," said Ashanty Bonilla, 17, a Mexican American high school junior in Idaho who faced so much ridicule from classmates last year that she transferred. "They hear it. They think it's okay. The president says it... Why can't they?" An online survey of over 10,000 kindergarten through 12th-grade educators by the Southern Poverty Law Center found that more than 2,500 "described specific incidents of bigotry and harassment that can be directly traced to election rhetoric"; although the statistic is overwhelming, the majority never made the news. In 476 cases, offenders used the phrase "build the wall." In 672, they mentioned deportation.

Poor civil leadership behavior example extends from rhetoric into action when examine how Texas tried to take the U.S. Supreme Court where it's never gone before with a lawsuit that sought to win a second term for President Donald Trump by overturning the election results in four other states carried by now President Joe Biden. Trump's effort to overturn the election results failed miserably when all nine Justices rejected the Texas long shot. Trump demanded the high court disenfranchise voters in four states and declare Trump the winner of the 2020 Election. Not only did over a dozen Republican state attorneys general join the lawsuit, 126 Republicans in the House signed off on it as well; therefore, they all sought to overthrow democracy and the Constitution in a betrayal of our country that constitutes treason.

Facebook, Instagram, and Twitter amplified Trump's uncivility. While I am a staunch supporter of Free Speech, I support the suspension of Donald Trump's social media accounts. Of course, there is a "free speech" aspect of their decision. Nonetheless, Trump's conduct, particularly his lies about the 2020 election, meet the constitutional definition of prohibited speech: "that which would be directed to and likely to incite imminent lawless action." Equally important is the notion that, as President of the United States, Donald Trump should not have been using his "bully pulpit" to foment uncivility; he should not have been undermining democracy.

Donald Trump's preferred style is to be uncivil. Trump's presidency was an expression of the insurgent's wish to "blow up" Washington. Donald railed against Washington "elites" and promised to "drain the swamp." He bragged about not being a politician, of bringing a different perspective into the oval office. Trump advertised himself as a political insurgent.

Of course, there's nothing wrong with looking at national politics from a different point of view. It's true that many feel that there are Washington elites who often do not promote the best interests of the American people but rather the power and fortune of the wealthy. Many Trump supporters voted for Donald because they truly believed that he would shake up Washington; that he would foment a populist revolution that would improve the life circumstances of his supporters. He didn't do that during his term in office.

The Trump presidency was not an era of finding new ways to promote the people's best interests but rather finding ways to promote Trump's interests. Donald Trump practiced the ultimate "bait and switch." He promised to "drain the swamp" but instead became the swamp and raised self-dealing to an art form. Trump promised to "end American carnage" but instead promoted violence with attacks on the press, people-of-color – most everyone other than white men – and political dissidents. Ultimately, Trump's rhetoric promoted the January 6th insurrection. Donald Trump blew up "political correctness" and replaced it with anger, insults, and lies with his uncivility. He demeaned gentility. He normalized what had previously been viewed as unacceptable behavior. Now is the time to step back from the abyss. Now is the time to defend civility. We must figure out ways to make political discourse in the United States government more civil. Civility matters.! Emotional Civility is key and is the moral framework for "civil society," without which Democracy cannot function. Civility is the heart-emotional civility is the way; and a civil society is the circulatory system.

Another area where emotional civility in leadership is critical is in the church and faith-based organizations, non-profit organizations and fraternities and sororities. It should not be taken for granted that because the organization is a church, or non-profit organization that is known for "doing good" that it is not fraught with a struggle to maintain emotionally civil behavior during governance meetings and generally in leadership. A church is made up of individuals- of human beings. Despite holding a position in the church (Pastor, Elder, Minister, Deacon), the same individuals may be struggling with emotionally charged challenges or stress outside of the church (self-esteem, marital, children, financial) that often surfaces in the midst of disagreements in a church setting. Moreover, there is a heavy burden that a church leader carries in helping others. There is an expectation from congregation that as a Pastor, or church leader, that you have no problems, and that as a leader you must always be ready to handle their problems- no matter what you are facing. Despite the fact that you may be grieving your mother's death - you are expected to show up and preach or serve at a congregation member's mother's funeral. Your husband may have left you - yet you are called on to give counsel and support to a marriage that is in jeopardy. That is the true call of ministry-and that is the burden we committed to carry if we are called and licensed and ordained. However, having held a leadership position in the church for over 20 years, I have seen leadership in many areas fail to model civil behavior or practice emotional civility when they are going through trying times in their own lives. The lack of civility oftentimes is related to stress outside of the church that the leader has not addressed. Transparent moment: there have been times when I have responded inappropriately in a church leadership setting due to issues and stress outside of the church that I have not fully managed-

and the residue of the outside issues crept into my responses as a leader. Emotional civility requires us to be cognizant of our emotions-especially as leaders- so we do model appropriate civil behavior. While as human beings we will make mistakes. However, I write this book and this chapter to remind my fellow colleagues of the cloth, that we have to engage in self-care in order to care for others. Unfortunately as Pastors, it can take weeks, months, even years to live down an emotional outburst, or angry reaction. Deacons and Ushers, you can drive a flock away from a church due to a frown, unfriendly tone, or an uncivil response to someone at the door of the church. We cannot take for granted that people will recover from how we treat them. In church we are in the people business, so we must pay careful attention to how we treat others. Again, emotional civility is horizontal and addresses the effect of our emotional reactions. We can only manage our emotional reactions if we work on ourselves. It is not automatic. Just being in church and attending church every week does not mean that we do not have to continuously work on ourselves. For Christians reading the bible and listening to the Word of God is critical-but only one step. Emotional civility requires that we must remain focused on where we are on the EC spectrum and know when we have to engage in self -care so that we can authentically be available to serve others with the love of God and civility.

In non-profit organizations, and sororities and fraternities we often see lack of civil behavior and cliques and bullying among members. While these organizations raise money and donate for noble causes and accomplish great work throughout the world; I have seen members fight for power in leadership and in the process tear down others just for the right to have the title "President". I have seen grown women in their 60s cry because of the treatment of their fellow members- simply because they disagreed with the budget for the annual "tea" event. I have seen grown men cuss and fight because they simply did not agree. In these instances – we are commanded to check our emotions and leave them at the door. In these settings, we as LEADERS are commanded to do better and be better.

We also see this fight for leadership and incivility in leadership in the military among initiation procedures and ranks. Recently, the US Military has come under fire for its treatment of people of color and women in its ranks. We must remember that dignity and respect are not simply the absence of discrimination and harassment. Demonstrating dignity and respect are actions-that, when applied consciously and consistently, create a culture of civility within an organization. Army Regulation 600-20, paragraph 5-13 states, "There is an indisputable link between how Soldiers are treated and how they perform their duties. Human relations training directly affects individual and unit readiness. Training commanders and Soldiers are required to treat one another with dignity and respect – [and that this conduct] achieves better morale, greater commitment, increased trust and cohesion, and better performance." In a 2018 interview for Army Reserve magazine, Matthew Burton, U.S. Army Reserve Command, senior Equal Employment Opportunity specialist at Fort McCoy, Wisconsin, explained why individuals might not always know what right looks like. "Education, training and awareness are important," Burton said. "Sometimes, because of their socialization and the culture they came from prior to being in the military or working as a government civilian, people might not be aware of their inappropriate behaviors. It's important to be trained on what dignity and respect looks like," Burton continued, "to be made aware of what right looks like. It's also important to make people aware of why they should maintain dignity and respect in the workplace." In today's professional environment it is necessary to know how your behavior effects those around you. Civility requires the ability to recognize other people's personal boundaries while maintaining boundaries of your own. Civility becomes increasingly imperative in the combined, joint, interagency, multi-national environments of today's Army Reserve workplaces and on the battlefields as well. Civility is not left behind when we deploy in support of combat operations. Civility and lethality are not mutually exclusive. "No matter what, it goes back to dignity and respect," Burton stated. "We have to create that environment and leaders have to model those behaviors of civility in the workplace. "Because at the end of the day," Burton said, "civility is necessary for the effectiveness of the organization."

Well-informed, well-trained, proactive organizations (Private, Faith-based, Non-profits, Military) should ensure its members understand not only how to show dignity and respect but why. In these times, and now more than ever, we are compelled to put emotional civility into practice. Leaders set the tone for the types of professional interactions expected by role-modeling civility, professionalism, and ethical conduct. This attitude resonates with Martin Buber's concept of the "I-You" connection, where two people are in rapport. These are the human moments when we feel fully engaged and contacted; these are the moments of personal connection we value the most. This is what allows for the chemistry where people can work together at their best. What then, does this take? In Social Intelligence Martin Buber described the varieties of empathy – cognitive, emotional, and empathic concern. These are prerequisites for the full engagement that allows deep emotional civility. But beyond that, each of us can take responsibility for conducting ourselves so the people we work with and leader, feel attuned to us. Given the countless distractions we face, this begins with paying full attention. The ingredients of a moment of human connection start with our putting down what we're doing, stopping our wandering thoughts, and simply paying full attention to another person. Particularly among those in the caring professions (Pastors, Doctors, Nurse, Social Workers), the ability to recover from such stress is crucial. The University of Massachusetts is home to a program in Mindfulness-based stress reduction. This training – which has spread to hundreds of hospitals and clinics – gives people the inner ability to stay calm and attuned without closing down to other people. In the emotional intelligence model, self-awareness and managing our emotions well are the keys to self-mastery. Once we stabilize in a positive state, we can become senders of that positivity to others. And that suggests one strategy for dealing with what may seem to be an obnoxious encounter – stay calm and clear, be firm but friendly. Because every interaction is a system, this can have a positive impact on the other person. And even if they do not change how they are acting, we can leave their negativity behind as we go on to the next encounter. In short, the ability to pass on to others our own positive state suggests a deeper sense of "civility."

This notion of "Civility at work" is more an exception rather than a rule for most work or volunteer environments. In that case, it is best to separate yourself from the situation before crafting a response to the person who is may and be delivering a rude comment. In this world of instant gratification and response, it is easy to bring in your own emotions and respond to soothe your ego, feel more important, show the upper hand, etc. But more often than not, you are adding gasoline to the fire and making matters worse. The best response in situations like this one is always a delayed but thoughtful response even at the cost of letting the other person feel like they won for that moment in time. This is true emotional civility and leaders must learn how to lead the way to a more civil society.

CHAPTER SIXTEEN

POLICE BRUTALITY

"When you have police officers who abuse citizens, you erode public confidence in law enforcement. That makes the job of good police officers unsafe" — Mary Frances Berry

L aw is defined by "a system of rules which a particular country or community recognizes as regulating the actions of its members and which it may enforce by the imposition of penalties." Therefore, each citizen of that community or country must be aware of these regulations and civics to understand their rights and act accordingly. However, it is troubling to find in my research that only 32 states as well as DC "provide instruction on American democracy, the history of the constitution and Bill of Rights; an explanation of mechanisms for public participation; and instruction on state and local voting policies" (Center of American Progress). This means 18 states, which is about 35% of the country, are not being educated on how their government works, the law, and most importantly how to vote. To put that in a deeper perspective, 35% of our country's population is 114,800,000 people. 114,800,000, at least (not counting the people who did not attend high school), were not educated on how our law works. These are people who hold a broad range of jobs from working in retail and food services to holding seats in congress and, most relevant to this chapter, our police forces. The first and most important thing you learn about in your government class is the Declaration of Independence. And in the second paragraph of the first article it reads, "We hold these Truths to be self-evident, that all men are created equal, that they are endowed by their Creator with certain unalienable Rights, that among these are Life, Liberty and the Pursuit of Happiness." All men are created equal meaning despite their color, gender, sexual orientation, religion, and social status they have rights that can never be denied nor taken away. A concept that is studied in our high school government classes for a year and police academies for 12-14 weeks. I believe this is problematic given the way we grow up ultimately affects the way we learn and receive information. It is problematic to wait until an individual becomes a legal adult and graduates high school to teach them important civics and governmental concepts. The individual has already made up what they believe is to be right and wrong; acting according to their own beliefs and morals. This is problematic for the child who grows up in a racist household and was taught that certain skin colors and ethnicities should be demeaned and feared. It is problematic for the child who is taught that because of someone's homosexual preferences they should not be given the same rights as everyone else. Or the child who was taught to believe only their religion held the right beliefs and other religions were ultimately radical because their beliefs were different. Imagine these same children going through the process of becoming police officers some 18-20 years later. The 12-14 weeks they are being taught civics and ethical practices cannot change a mindset that has been nurtured and programmed throughout childhood to adulthood. For example, it is like when you study world religions in high school.

Most people do not listen to the concept of the world religion to understand, they listen to pass the class and get the grade. Their brains mostly skim over information because it serves no purpose to them to retain it. That is how it would feel for someone who goes into the police academy who was not taught the holistic approach of ethics but only for a certain demographic of people. They will most likely learn the information to pass the academy, but not to understand or retain it. Another thing that is not required in 49 of our states that is problematic is community service. It is recommended but not at all required. For someone looking to become a police officer to have not done any community service prior to their duty as an officer is inconceivable. How can someone learn to empathize with a community and a group of people they have never been around before? If all a person has known is where and how they grew up, they will fail to serve different communities effectively because they have never immersed themselves in another community. Someone who was taught and grew up with the notion that certain communities and neighborhoods should be avoided will consequently nurture a biased fear that they will still have if they choose to become a police officer. How can you serve and protect a community you were taught to fear? Ultimately one has been nurtured with a reflex of defensiveness instead of ethics, empathy, understanding, and sometimes law.

Police Brutality has run rampant in our American system and has its roots deeply ingrained in our American society. It has caused the issue of Emotional Civility to be highlighted and the need to respond and train officers not solely on proper responses, NOT just based on their conduct.

Emotional Civility

Perspective-taking is reflective of the metaphor "stepping inside someone else's shoes," which is perceiving a situation in an alternative point of view to ultimately achieve empathy. It is a scientific fact that Perspective-taking leads others to feel 78% more empathetic towards others. Seventy-eight percent is a lot more than 0% and could be a great incentive to include Perspective-taking in police training. A lot of people mistake Perspective-taking for sympathy or active listening. Perspective-taking differs from sympathy because it is not emotionally based. You can feel sorrow for someone, but it is ultimately determined by what and who you think deserves that sympathy. With active listening, the focus is more on solving disputes and conflict between two people who already know each other. Active listening is to concentrate and understand what is being told so you can properly respond verbally. However, in situations of police brutality where there is no pre-existing knowledge of that person's background, where the police are not familiar with the person they are addressing, sympathy and active listening are out of reach. To be able to provide sympathy and correctly follow through with active listening a person must first acknowledge that the person deserves that level of respect. I believe the best way to achieve Perspective-taking is for police to learn about the communities and the citizens they are serving to protect.

Perspective-taking will establish a foundation of respect, sympathy, and mutual understanding. Another technique is temporal distancing. Temporal distancing helps immediately reduce negative emotions and make tough conversations more productive by focusing on the desired outcome. If we can focus on the desired outcome instead of everything that could go wrong, we take away any regretful impulsive behaviors based on that negativity. This also can be done through structured listening. Structured listening is so much more powerful and effective than active listening because it is forcing each speaker to step in the others' point of view. With this technique, the goal is that each side of the conversation gains newfound knowledge from each other. Unlike active listening, structured listening takes turns with who is the speaker and listener throughout the talk. It also is more focused and interested in what the other person has to say than getting their point across. Instead of saying "I believe" the statements are more centered around "tell me more about A B C." The three steps to effective structured listening are eliciting, listening, and confirming. Eliciting is simply making a statement with the purpose of evoking a response out of someone. In structured listening this is effective because it gives the listener an invitation to talk about something they might've been uncomfortable with talking about. The intention is to build a foundation of trust, so the speaker is comfortable with expressing themselves. Once you build a foundation of trust and security in the conversation the objective is to simply listen in order to confirm what the speaker has said. Confirmation is also a form of acknowledgment of what has been spoken and further retained.

In the wake of George Floyd's death and the subsequent protests worldwide, virtually every company is starting to engage in some very, difficult conversations. The conversations everyone is having, however, are centered around one word: "why?". Why does an innocent 12-year-old boy playing in the park with a toy gun lead up to him being shot dead multiple times? Why does an innocent 17-year-old boy with a hoodie on and skittles in his hand pose enough threat to be shot in the back while walking home? Or what about the woman who had violated curfew in the Doe v. Marsalis case. Why was she taken to the officer's house, where he raped her while holding her at gunpoint, instead of the station? And most recently, why was a man who continuously yelled out he could not breathe with a foot on his neck ignored by police officers and the ambulance for 5mn and 53 seconds resulting in his death. Why haven't Breyonna Taylor's murderers been convicted when they "mistakenly" shot her after breaking into her house without a warrant or cause; but only because they thought they had the right house? All these questions are questions that we should never have to ask as human beings. Nothing justifies an unjust killing and nothing justifies a life being taken by "mistake." Making a mistake is like forgetting your work at home, spilling coffee on your pants, or mixing up someone's order. A mistake should never be considered taking someone's life on a threat one has presumed. Police brutality has been highlighted because most victims have been African Americans and the perpetrators white. So, the answer we have been given to these questions is racism. However, no one is born racist, so we look further into what separates a black man from a white man. Why does the color of a black man's skin automatically put him in a life-or-death situation when approached by a cop? People tend to forget what the word victim means when it comes to a person of color falling victim to police brutality, but it's simple. Somehow these officers have created an image of violence and oppression among the African American community. To them black automatically poses a threat. A generational brainwashed concept that has been here since slavery. And although we are angered by the ignorance, blatant disrespect, negligence, and racism, we must focus on the root of the issue and learn how to plant our seeds differently. The seeds in this case that need to be planted are emotional civility. If these officers were trained on perspective-taking, active listening, temporal distancing, structured listening, and eliciting techniques as listed above all those that have fallen victim to police brutality would be alive right now. It doesn't just start with the perpetrators but us, too, taking the responsibility to educate everyone on those techniques and spread knowledge and love rather than hate. Love for your fellow human being makes civil responses so much easier.

CHAPTER SEVENTEEN

EMOTIONAL CIVILITY IN THE FAMILY

"Aspire to decency. Practice civility toward one another. Admire and emulate ethical behavior wherever you find it. Apply a rigid standard of morality to your lives; and if, periodically, you fail - as you surely will - adjust your lives, not the standards."— Ted Koppel

How many of us have a mother or father that have told us to "fix your face"? The mantra, often hailed among African American parents, was offered when, as children, we could not or would not dare to express how we felt about something, but our body language and non-verbal cues spoke for us; often more loudly than words could ever speak. When evaluating our civility barometer, we must remember that IT'S NOT JUST WHAT YOU SAY, or how you say it, but IT'S WHAT YOU DO NOT SAY.

Taking the matter, a step further, what does it mean to have a family? I think we can all agree that the dictionary definition of "the basic unit in society traditionally consisting of two parents rearing their children" is shortsighted. Although that can be true, a family is ultimately built on the foundations of trust, security, comfort, and emotional civility among a group of people. Unfortunately, blood relation is not a guarantee that one is born into a family. For example, in the U.S, "A federal study has found that at least 22,000 babies are left in hospitals each year by parents unwilling or unable to care for them." With no access to the "traditional family," 22,000 children a year are dependent on anyone who can offer them trust, security, comfort, and emotional stability. All these things add up to a healthy family, attribute to the child's success, and equip them to ultimately survive our society. Trust is an important foundation because it establishes reliability and honesty between two or more people. Without trust, family members will feel alone and uncomfortable with expressing their emotions. They will then develop trust issues outside the family preventing them from taking any opportunities and exploring interests. Trust also plays a big part in emotional stability because it allows you to appropriately express your emotions. Security also plays a big part in a family because it is important to be able to feel safe around one another. A lack of security within one's family can nurture unhealthy defense mechanisms, coping mechanisms, and a lack of faith in people. This plays a part in emotional stability because when one does not feel safe their emotions can easily become uncontrollable. Comfort goes along with security but specifically details being comfortable in your skin around others. When one is not made comfortable in their skin within their family, it is mentally debilitating. Essentially, a family member or members are nurturing or reinforcing insecurities upon one another that stick for life. Consequently, this creates emotional instability because insecurities prevent a person from expressing their emotions at all or appropriately. Some people cannot control the unhealthy families they are born into or their rough background and, essentially, are forced to take the bare minimum. They accept that bad treatment is not only what they deserve but what they will always have. This makes it confusing when entering new relationships where their unhealthy mindsets are challenged, moving them to a place of discomfort and confusion. That's why it is important to treat everyone around us like family despite any lack of pre-existent bonds or blood relations. Just as Jesus did, we should strive to see everyone as brothers and sisters despite their color, race, sexual orientation, religion, beliefs, or social status. This will combat anyone affected by an unhealthy relationship or family they were natured in. I truly believe if we acted in this way, we could prevent gang violence, substance abuse, cyberbullying, and suicide among our children. Most children who have gone through these lack emotional stability, which is nurtured by living or being born into unhealthy environments and families. It is the simple fact that if a child does not feel loved or validated, they will not expect anyone to care about their mistakes or feelings nor do they care about others' feelings, ultimately lacking emotional stability. Emotional Civility is critical as we continue to build from the pandemic and emerge from social isolation. It is emotional civility that will build the bridges from the separation that the quarantine has created.

CHAPTER EIGHTEEN

THE ROLE OF FAITH: BACK TO BASICS – THE GOLDEN RULE

"Use empathy, thoughtfulness and kindness in your interactions and think before you speak. A kind word is long remembered."— Cindy Ann Peterson

The Golden Rule is the principle of treating others as you want to be treated. It is a maxim that is found in most religions and cultures. It can be considered an ethic or reciprocity. "Do unto others as you would have them do unto you" is the idea (also called the *law of reciprocity*) that may be the most universally applauded moral principle on Earth – the Golden Rule. Something like it appears in every major religion and ethical philosophy. The wording above is from the King James *Bible*, Matthew 7:12; however, Hindu, Jewish, Buddhist, Confucian, and Zoroastrian versions of it appeared 3,000-5,000 years earlier. The "Golden Rule" of Leviticus 19:18 was quoted by Jesus in Matthew 7:12 and described by him as the second great commandment. The Golden Rule is stated numerous times in the Old Testament:

Emotional Civility

Leviticus 9:18 ("Thou shalt not avenge, nor bear any grudge against the children of thy people, but thou shalt love thy neighbor as thyself: I am the LORD.") and Leviticus 19:34 ("But treat them just as you treat your own citizens. Love foreigners as you love yourselves because you were foreigners one time in Egypt. I am the Lord your God."), for example.

Our faith is a set of values for what we believe the world should be. As long as we continue to carry out those values and our work doesn't conflict with those values, then we can know that we are working for our own values. Faith should guide our work and the way we do our work. For Christians "what would Jesus do" guides or should guide how we respond. How we interact with other people, and how our faith dictates that interaction should be at the forefront of all the decisions we make and all the interactions we have. All religions promote civility! There is not one religion that tells us to treat people with hostility.

True Civility crosses boldly all lines of religion and denominations. True emotional civility welcomes a diverse conversation without the need for violence and condemnation. I am an Executive Pastor at a non-denominational church in Washington, DC. My faith and belief in Jesus Christ compel me to love not to hate. My faith compels me to look at the perspective of another. To disagree without crucifying someone who thinks differently, thus crucifying Jesus afresh. It was a difference of opinion and perspective that killed Christ. The political leaders feared Jesus and his different perspective. We cannot continue to fight against hate and embrace love if we want a better way for our world. However, the truth is that religion evokes intense responses because it plays an essential role in our lives. Our beliefs reflect who we are, what we care about, our purpose guides us. Inter-faith dialogue is hard, but intra-faith can be harder. Every Christian claims Jesus, so essential questions of how we understand Jesus, his earthly ministry, the meaning of the crucifixion, the nature of his call upon our lives (questions to which a non-Christian is largely indifferent) become the grounds of our essential debate and, literally, a matter of life and death. When we encounter a Christian, who thinks and believes differently, we experience that difference as an attack on the principles upon which we have built our lives and as a betrayal to the faith. This feeling only increases when you add in politics. In recent elections, both sides of the political aisle found inspiration and legitimization from Christian constituencies. Political debates often adopted theological rhetoric, and religious leaders adopted political strategies. The result has been a "winner take all" attitude with Christian groups being particularly brutal toward one another. These battles are not new.

Therefore, the call for civility begins again today and with each one of us. Christian Civility doesn't work if it is reduced pointing the finger at someone else and demanding them to be more civil.

Because civility and the barbaric history of the process of civilization in American history and culture has its roots in Christian religious ideation, it is often hard to begin to have the discussion of civility because it is seen as a silencing—it is seen as a taking over of free thought- it is seen as a crushing of individuality and diversity. As we move toward a more civil world- we must reject all forms of prejudice and discrimination, including those based on race, gender, gender identity, sexual orientation, privilege, or any other differences that have led to misunderstanding, hostility, and injustice- WORLDWIDE. Civility requires that we welcome diversity of thought and political beliefs. Basic principles of positive conflict resolution require that we treat one another with courtesy, mutual respect, and civility; even when we don't agree or understand. As we launch this new paradigm – it will be my goal to ensure that faith becomes the banner and hallmark for civility not the cause for the chilling effect on difference and speech.

CHAPTER NINETEEN

THE PERSONAL CONSEQUENCE OF EMOTIONAL INCIVILITY AND WAYS TO ADDRESS IT.

"The mentality of retaliation destroys states, while the mentality of tolerance builds nations." — Nelson Mandela.

In reviewing the cost of incivility there are personal consequences and certainly an impact on our society nationally and globally. When we fail to act with emotional civility:

- CREATIVITY SUFFERS

- PERFORMANCE AND TEAM SPIRIT DETERIORATE

- CONSUMERS TURN AWAY

- ITS EXPENSIVE BASED ON THE TIME IT TAKES TO REPAIR RELATIONSHIPS

- MOOD MATTERS

- OUTCOMES AND PROCESS MATTER

- ARE OPINIONS REQUESTED AND GIVEN SERIOUS CONSIDERATION?

- ARE DECISION MAKING PROCESSES TRANSPARENT?

- IS EVERYONE TREATED RESPECTFULLY?

- ARE LEADERS ACTIVELY LISTENING TO CONCERNS AND EMPATHIZING WITH THEIR POINT OF VIEW?

The cost to us and our future is too great to allow us to fail to examine how much emotional civility matters.

- HIT THE RESET BUTTON

- MOOD MATTERS

- OUTCOMES AND PROCESS MATTER

- IMAGINE YOUR IDEAL SELF—COMING TO TERMS WITH YOUR REAL SELF AS OTHERS EXPERIENCE YOU.....

- HOW DO YOU WANT PEOPLE TO PERCEIVE YOU?

- HOW ARE PEOPLE EXPERIENCING YOU?

- WHAT ADJUSTMENTS DO YOU NEED TO MAKE?

SUGGESTIONS ON PRACTICING EMOTIONAL CIVILITY

- CHOOSE TO SEE YOURSELF GREAT

- CHOOSE TO UNDERSTAND YOU DON'T HAVE TO RESPOND TO EVERYTHING

- CHOOSE TO KNOW YOUR WORTH

- CHOOSE TO CULTIVATE YOUR PEACE

- IT IS CRTIICAL TO CONSTANTLY ASSESS AND ADJUST OUR PERPECTIVE TO MAINTAIN PEACE AND TO MANIFEST PEACE AND CIVILITY IN ATTITUDE AND DISCOURSE

OBSERVE HOW YOU REACT TO PEOPLE.

- DO YOU RUSH TO JUDGMENT BEFORE YOU KNOW ALL OF THE FACTS?

- DO YOU STEREOTYPE YOUR REACTION TO PEOPLE BASED ON WHAT YOU HAVE HEARD?

- DO YOU UNDERSTAND THAT EVERYTHING DOES NOT NEED A RESPONSE?

LOOK AT YOUR ENVIRONMENT

DO YOU SEEK ATTENTION FOR YOUR ACCOMPLISHMENTS, OR DO YOU ACT WITH HUMILITY?

DO A SELF-EVALUATION

- WHAT ARE YOUR WEAKNESSES?

- ARE YOU WILLING TO ACCEPT THAT YOU ARE NOT PERFECT?

- CHAOS WILL HAPPEN BUT HOW WE RESPOND TO IT IS WHAT ENHANCES OR THREATENS OUR PEACE.

- KNOW WHERE YOU ARE AND TRULY STUDY EMOTIONAL INTELLIGENCE MODELS TO GAUGE WHERE YOU ARE ON THE CIVILITY SPECTRUM.

- DETACH FROM SOCIAL MEDIA

- TAKE A WALK

- LISTEN TO MUSIC THAT RELAXES OR UPLIFTS YOU

Helpful operational definitions of civil behaviors that we may wish to encourage, embrace, and reinforce include:

- THINKING BEFORE SPEAKING

- FOCUS ON FACTS RATHER THAN BELIEFS AND OPINIONS

- FOCUS ON THE COMMON GOOD RATHER THAN INDIVIDUAL AGENDAS

- DISAGREE WITH OTHERS RESPECTFULLY

- BE OPEN TO OTHERS WITHOUT HOSTILITY

- BE RESPECTFUL OF DIVERSE VIEWS AND GROUPS

- FOSTER A SPIRIT OF COLLEGIALITY

- OFFER PRODUCTIVE AND CORRECTIVE FEEDBACK TO THOSE WHO BEHAVE IN DEMEANING, INSULTING, DISRESPECTFUL, AND DISCRIMINATORY WAYS

Forms of uncivil behavior that should be avoided include the following:

- INTERRUPTING AND TALKING OVER OTHERS WHO HAVE THE FLOOR

- INSULTS AS WELL AS OVERGENERALIZED AND DISPOSITIONAL CHARACTER CRITICISMS AND ATTRIBUTIONS

- USE OF AGGRESSIVE, SARCASTIC, OR DEMEANING LANGUAGE AND TONE

- REFUSAL TO ACKNOWLEDGE THE GOOD POINTS OF OTHERS

Sometimes we can block our own blessings by not speaking up or embracing our current situation then taking steps to improve it.

We'd rather sink behind the scenes than to seek help. I learned that in order to grow we have to let our pride go and start standing in our truths as ugly or as bad as they may be. The only way to get better is to address those challenges that interfere with successful interaction in all spheres.

The old adage is true – a closed mouth doesn't get fed; in order to get what you want you have to begin to open your mouth and ask for it... the worst you can get is a no and the best is a yes. However, it is always the way we ask and how we process the no and respond to the no. I have mentored hundreds of people because someone poured into me. Someone saw potential in me and regardless of the mistakes that I made in life. Through it all God made a way because I got out of my comfort zone, because I wanted more for me.

Emotional Civility

Nobody had to make me want to change, because my will to succeed grew stronger than my will to stay the same!!!. If I can do it so can you – get determined and laser focused. Work for a cause not for applause; live life to express not to impress; don't strive to make your presence noticed just make your absence felt. Stay humble, be teachable, and always keep learning.

One area of everyday life in which to practice civility is that of conversation. A civil discussion is the free and respectful exchange of diverse ideas. This doesn't mean we all have to agree, but it does mean we must agree respectfully. To paraphrase Justice Stewart, "I'm not sure what it is, but I know it when I see it;" or don't see it as the case may be around the world.

CHAPTER TWENTY

WHY NOW? WHY THE NEW STANDARD OF GLOBAL SUCCESS?

"Civic charity is easy to talk about but tremendously difficult to practice - mainly because a lot of people don't reciprocate-but there is hope for our future if we all commit to change"— Sharon Anderson

Civility is the engine on which the world runs. If there is a time when we need to be reminded of the need for civil discourse it is now. When I began writing this book, we were on the brink of war with Iran, our 45th President was in the midst of impeachment hearings, and a hearing for his removal was pending. I waited to finish the book, and then on January 6, 2020 we watched as a mob of Trump supporters unhappy with the outcome of the 2020 election staged a coup and desecrated our Capitol. We have seen over, and over again Black men killed at the hands of those who have been paid to protect and serve us. There are protests all over the World against Police Brutality. Black on Black crime has risen. We are also in the midst of an election where our current President is name calling and provoking racist and uncivil discourse.

Emotional Civility

Emotional Civility day is on March 6, 2021. Participation is open to all people of the world. People may choose to celebrate EC Day in different ways, but the goal is to have civil interaction and discourse at the heart of all the activity's intentions. Individuals, businesses, and organizations are also welcome and encouraged to celebrate EC. Engaging in civil interaction is the great aim that's in view for raising awareness for Emotional Civility Day.

What is undisputed is that Incivility is all around us, it is a global problem, a human problem, a moral problem, and if left unchecked, it may become so much a part of our moral fabric that it can't be reversed. Because Civility is a HUMAN ISSUE AND A MORAL ISSUE-Everything you hear during this conference or are about to hear during this conference has at its foundation what I have termed "Emotional Civility". Emotional Civility is the root of authentic civility and requires us to dig deep to uncover anything that prevents us from reacting and acting with civility.

Authentic and lasting civility requires that we take a self-inventory, and it is only through self-evaluation that we can effectively correct the course of the deep-seated incivility that our world is experiencing. Because civility is a human issue and not an esoteric concept-our something we just read about-we must understand that Individual emotions can be a contributing barrier to collective worldwide civility. The emotional civility paradigm encourages all of us to find ways to break down and prevent our own emotional barriers to true civil interaction.

Finally, Emotional Civility recognizes that disparities exist but intentionally looks to build bridges and promotes and facilitates communication that addresses the attitudes and consequences of that disparity, thus leading to harmonious change and a sustainably civil society shared and enjoyed by all.

As mentioned before and worth noting again, there is a bridge that is built between individuals when the communicate and apply emotional civility that ensures emotionally civil responses and interaction. That bridge can be built with understanding, tolerance, and the components of civility. That bridge can also be obliterated with the issues that undermine true civility for all (racism, misogyny, privilege, and inequality). The concept and practice of civility cannot silence opinions and beliefs. It requires openness. Self-absorption, pride, prejudice, bigotry, low self-esteem are all barriers to civility. We must talk time to hear each other out. We must learn to debate without losing our tempers. We must commit to vigorous exchanges about matters without taking offense – simply because someone does not agree. Our interdependence is the rule and not the exception. It is essential for us to have a sincere insight into ourselves, and take the time to understand each other, which should lead to sustainable civility resulting in harmonious existence.

In assessing the barriers to civility -emotional civility encourages us all to work on our individual processing of information as we work to ensure our responses are authentic and civil and promote positive and lasting change for all. The difference between equity and equality must be considered in analyzing the impact of our responses and whether we are engaging in emotional civility. It is only by addressing the roots causes of incivility and unmasking or removing the band-aides that prevent us from having transparent discussions, that we can truly begin to address the barriers to civility and develop meaningful solutions. Just as the removing a band aide from a healing scab or open wound can be a painful – removing the band-aides from the areas that create a wall to civil communications can cause discomfort.

Without the ability to engage in difficult conversations, it is impossible to advance ideas, progress, or embrace free expression of thought and speech. It is the intertwining of humanity that requires an open mind in order to achieve civil discourse.

❖ Breaking the Barriers of Civility requires that we welcome diversity of thought and political beliefs.

❖ Breaking the Barriers of Civility requires that we use basic principles of positive conflict resolution.

❖ Breaking the Barriers of Civility requires that we treat one another with courtesy, mutual respect, and civility; even when we don't agree or understand.

❖ Breaking the Barriers of Civility requires that we have to be willing to listen.

❖ Breaking the Barriers of Civility requires that we have to move past our own biases.

The barriers of unspoken and inherent biases must be broken for true civility to prevail. We must reject all forms of prejudice and discrimination, including those based on race, gender, gender identity, sexual orientation, privilege, or any other differences that have led to misunderstanding, hostility, and injustice-WORLDWIDE.

Not everyone will respond with civility to civility. But my goal as a thought leader and civility scholar, is to encourage us all to continue to use civility and make an effort to respond with civility – even in the face of the harshest circumstances. We need to begin to think of civility as continual and non-negotiable. It is not something that we turn off and on.

Commitment to do what is right must prevail in our society. Civil policies must be created, and we cannot simply offer lip service to those situations that require civility. We cannot use an old environment for new policies. Difference in opinion will occur, but we must remember that diversity is not adversity. We must cry out for civility over uniformity. All too often we underestimate the power and virtue of civility. Words matter, words empower, words create. We must choose them wisely. Emotional Civility requires that you intentionally understand and are conscious of the effect your words have on others. The more power you have or position you have – the more conscious you must be about their effect. We all know the superhero Marvel studios famous mantra—With great power comes great responsibility. Passionate emotions must be harnessed and channeled through good manners and etiquette to civilize any debate in our diverse society. Reckless and malicious expressions will lead to vilification and continuous destruction of each other and our communities.

CONCLUSION

We recognize that individual or collective human dignity is a fundamental right and that the desecration of such through insult, denigration or humiliation is morally and ethically wrong. Passionate emotions must be harnessed and channeled through good manners and etiquette to civilize any debate in our diverse society. Reckless and malicious expressions will lead to vilification and demonstration of each other and our communities. Our interdependence is the rule and not the exception. It is essential for us to have a sincere insight into each other, which should lead to sustainable civility resulting in harmonious existence. Challenges we face in negotiating differences are far greater than those that were faced by civilizations of the past.

Every day we are presented with opportunities to interact on a variety of levels with different individuals and groups. Each one of these interactions is important to the person or persons on the receiving end of our communication and our actions. Let's work hard – and with intentionality – to be part of a community where everyone feels valued and respected. Together, we are the community, and we are building on a long legacy of civility and responsibility. The future is in our hands, as is that legacy, and we can continue to strengthen both by modeling the values of the Golden Rule.

I hope partnering with our ongoing investigation of this critically important issue can help in at least a small way to restore civility in public life and bring meaningful and long-lasting solutions to our ways of interacting and behaving in all aspects of American life. When you treat people with civility you get a civil future. I believe that we can build a civil future for our children and their children. Will you help me? As you begin to think about your own path to emotional civility, please consider the following Self Reflection Questions:

- How do you define civility?

- Is civility common or individualized?

- Have you ever wrestled with acting in a civil manner?

- What are your triggers?

- Was there a time when you realized that you could and should improve on your responses?

- If so – what was the defining moment?

- Do you think it is at all important to exercise restraint when communicating?

What is clear is that the nation's institutions must play a role. Americans are decidedly open to institutional involvement in addressing the country's civility deficit. Americans believe there is a larger role for many institutions to play in helping improve the level of civility in our nation, including government, media, educational, and business entities. Very few want less involvement from any institution, which is interesting, since some, including social media and government officials, are seen as drivers of incivility. Clearly, everyone is expected to take ownership for their own contributions to this crisis and change the course of its trajectory.

Combining those efforts with other institutions — including government entities, religious groups, businesses, and educational bodies —will bring diverse points of view to bear on developing solutions. A National Civility Day shows some promise, and a broader campaign could incorporate awards for outstanding acts of civility conferred by Congress or a media outlet. It would be important to enlist political forces in this initiative, perhaps at a more local level, to connect members of opposing parties and offer support for a constructive exchange of ideas. That is why I applied to the National archives and was awarded National Emotional Civility Day.

Finally, these programs should all be designed around empowering the individual to get involved. Americans are willing to take action and contribute greater civility in their day-to-day conduct. Communicators can offer tools through social media, as well as through traditional and local outlets, to foster positive dialogue and celebrate good deeds. Mobilizing Civility Advocates and supplying them with actionable programs for promoting civility in their communities would be effective in advancing a nationwide civility initiative.

The future of global success truly does lie in civility. If we hope to create a brighter and more efficient future for later generations and ourselves, just as our founding fathers so desired, then we must possess two qualities: hope and civility.

I challenge everyone reading this book to continue to work hard – and with conscious intentionality – to be part of a community where everyone feels valued and respected. Together, we are the community, and we are building on a long legacy of civility and responsibility. Together we can break down the barriers that block us from living in a more civil nation and world. Emotional Civility is the foundation of Civility for all.

** All statistics found within this book are from Weber Shandwick and KRC research on Civility Nationwide. **